THE LEGENDS OF
STOKE CITY

THE LEGENDS OF
STOKE CITY
1863-2008

Tony Matthews

DB
PUBLISHING

First published in Great Britain in 2008 by
The Breedon Books Publishing Company Limited
Breedon House, 3 The Parker Centre,
Derby, DE21 4SZ.

Paperback edition published in Great Britain in 2012 by
The Derby Books Publishing Company Limited,
3 The Parker Centre, Derby, DE21 4SZ.

ISBN 978-1-78091-139-7

Printed and bound by Copytech (UK) Limited, Peterborough.

Contents

Acknowledgements

First and foremost, I would like to say a special thank you to Steve Caron, managing director of Breedon Books Publishing, who agreed to publish this book, and also to the company's editor Michelle Grainger and junior editor Alex Morton.

Also thank you to Stoke City supporters Julian Boodell and Peter Wyatt for supplying most of the photographs, to Melissa Gray for clarifying certain dates appertaining to the birth and death of players, and to Stoke City Football Club.

And I cannot forget my darling wife, Margaret, for all the help, support and encouragement that she has given me as always. It is getting something of a habit saying this, but compiling all these football books is quite enjoyable, really!

Note

As stated, the majority of pictures used in this book have come from supporters. Some have come from other sources, and in this respect it has been hard to establish clear copyright on quite a few of these pictures. Therefore, both I and the publishers – Breedon Books Publishing – would be pleased to hear from anyone whose copyright has unintentionally been infringed.

Notes on the text

On the following pages, you will find multitudinous, authentic personal details of 100 star players who have appeared for Stoke City football club over a long period of time. Throughout the book, I have referred to the club as either (a) Stoke, (b) Stoke City or (c) the Potters, regardless of the year.

The appearance and goalscoring records for each player cover all major competitions, including the Championship (2004–08); the Football League, Divisions One, Two, Three and Three North (1893–2004); the FA Cup (1883–2008); the League Cup, in its various guises (1960–2008); the Fairs Cup and UEFA Cup. There are also details appertaining to the Anglo-Italian Cup, the Anglo-Scottish Cup, the Autoglass Trophy, Auto Windscreen Shield and Zenith Data Systems Cup tournaments, while all records relating to World War One and Two have also been included where applicable.

Figures that appear after the + sign in reference to a player's personal record indicate the number of substitute appearances he made for the club. All the statistics are deemed to be correct up to the end of the 2007–08 season.

Where a single year appears in the text (when referring to an individual player's career), this indicates, in most cases, the second half of a season: for example, 1975 refers to the 1974–75 season. However, when the dates appear as 1975–80, this refers to seasons 1975–76 to 1979–80 inclusive and not 1974–75 to 1980–81.

If you spot any discrepancies, errors, even omissions, I would appreciate it very much if you could contact me (via the publishers) so that all can be amended in any future publications regarding Stoke City Football Club. If you have anything to add, this would also be appreciated and most welcome, as people often reveal unknown facts from all sorts of sources when football is the topic of conversation.

Introduction

To choose 100 legends from any club that has been in existence for over 140 years is no easy task, believe you me. Therefore, I am certainly expecting a few supporters, young and old, to ask the question: why was his or her favourite player not included? If I had been allowed to feature 200 star players, past and present, there would not have been a problem and no worries about missing anyone out and upsetting any diehard Potters fans. But that was not the case, and I had to select 100 out of the 800 or so players who have served the club since its formation way back in 1863.

I have concentrated, in the main, on players who spent some time as a Stoke City footballer, all-time greats who accumulated superb records in terms of appearances made as well as goals scored, such as: Gordon Banks, Alan Bloor, Frank Bowyer, Terry Conroy, Peter Dobing, Alan Dodd, George Eastham, Neil Franklin, Tom Holford, Jock Kirton, John McCue, Sir Stanley Matthews, Bob McGrory, Frank Mountford, Harry Oscroft, John Ritchie, Joe Schofield, Harry and Johnny Sellars, Eric Skeels, Denis Smith, Freddie Steele, Arthur Turner, Dennis Viollet and Charlie Wilson. And I have included as well one of the club's greatest-ever managers, Tony Waddington.

All I can say is that the 100 players – the legends – featured in this book gave Stoke City Football Club and its supporters a great deal to cheer about over the course of time.

Read and enjoy.

Tony Matthews, August 2008

Tony Allen

Born:	27 November 1939, Stoke-on-Trent

Stoke City record:

Appearances:	League 414+3, FA Cup 30, League Cup 26
Goals:	League 2, FA Cup 1, League Cup 1
Debut:	League, 14 December 1957 v Doncaster Rovers (a) won 1–0
Also played for:	Hellenic (South Africa), Stafford Rangers, England (4 Youth, 7 Under-23 and 3 full caps)

Born shortly after the outbreak of World War Two, Tony Allen, with his distinctive blond hair, was a splendid left-back, sure-footed with a fine tackle and temperament. He appeared in well over 470 games for Stoke City during the 1950s and 1960s, helping the team win the Second Division Championship in 1962–63 and reach the League Cup Final the following year, when they lost over two legs to Leicester City. Capped three times by England, he left the Victoria Ground in 1970, signing for Bury for £10,000. Later he went to South Africa to play for Hellenic FC before returning to live and work in the Potteries in the 1980s, when he occasionally assisted Stafford Rangers.

An England Youth international before he bedded himself into the Potters' first team, Tony went on to gain his first full cap against Wales at Ninian Park, Cardiff, a month before his 20th birthday. He deputised for the injured Jimmy Armfield in the 1–1 draw and retained his place for the next two games, partnering West Bromwich Albion's Don Howe at full-back against Sweden at Wembley (lost 3–2) and against Northern Ireland in Belfast (won 2–1).

Besides his intermediate and senior outings for England, Tony also represented the Football League on two occasions and, at the time, was rated one of the best four full-backs in the country. Unfortunately he could not dislodge Armfield or his successor Ray Wilson and, as a result, missed out on the 1962 World Cup in Chile – although he was named as a stand-by reserve until the final list of players was submitted.

A pupil at Broom Street and Wellington Road schools (where Stanley Matthews was also educated), Tony was a member of the local Boys' Brigade. He joined Stoke City as an amateur in April 1955 and turned professional in November 1956. He effectively took over from John McCue at left-back in the Stoke side, while McCue switched flanks. A great first season saw him gain 34 League appearances in 1957–58, adding a further 36 to his tally in 1958–59 and 39 the following season before having two ever-present campaigns, during which time he was joined at full-back by Tim Ward and then Bill Asprey.

Tony was outstanding in 1962–63 when the Potters won the Second Division title. He missed only one game (against Preston) and produced some exquisite performances down the left, assisting winger Don Ratcliffe whenever possible and delivering some teasing crosses into the danger zone with his immaculate left foot.

He made his bow in the First Division on the opening day of the 1963–64 season in front of more than 40,000 fans at the Victoria Ground, when Stoke beat Tottenham Hotspur 2–1. Continuing to play exceptionally well, he missed only one game that season and was a key figure as the Potters reached the League Cup Final. Unfortunately, after a 1–1 first-leg draw at home to Leicester City, Stoke lost the return game at Filbert Street 3–2 and finished runners-up after going down 4–3 on aggregate.

Towards the end of 1964–65 Tony received an injury and was out of the team for six months. He returned in November 1965 but was never the same player again and in fact his manager (Tony Waddington) moved him into a central-defensive position alongside Alan Bloor, with Eric Skeels bedding down at left-back. Tony did well in his new role and had a superb 1967–68 season but, disappointingly, he was in and out of the side afterwards and eventually moved to pastures new, joining Bury. He later assisted the South African club Hellenic before returning to England, where he wound down his playing days with non-League side Stafford Rangers.

In later life, Tony went into business in his native Potteries.

Bobby Archibald

Born: 6 November 1894, Strathaven, Lanarkshire
Died: 8 January 1966, Glasgow

Stoke City record:
Appearances: League 262, FA Cup 14
Goals: League 37, FA Cup 3
Debut: League, 29 August 1925 v Stockport County (h) won 3–0

Also played for: Rutherglen Glencairn, Glasgow Rangers (amateur), Albion
                     Rovers (two spells), Aberdeen, Third Lanark (two spells), Barnsley

A diminutive Scottish-born left-winger, Robert (Bobby) Franklin Archibald made a dream start to his career with Stoke City, scoring on his debut for the Potters in a 3–0 home win over Stockport County at the start of the 1925–26 campaign.

Stoke had used no less than eight players on the left flank during the previous season so the arrival of Bobby was a breath of fresh air to the club and indeed to the supporters.

Bobby quickly became an established member of the side and went on to appear in 276 games for the club, netting 40 goals. He gained a Third Division North League Championship-winners' medal at the end of his second season at the Victoria Ground and, after giving the Potters excellent and dedicated service for seven full years, he switched his allegiance to Barnsley in the summer of 1932, having struggled with injury and seen Tim Maloney, Harry Taylor and future England international Joe Johnson also deputise for him on the left wing.

Often referred to as 'Steve' by his teammates because he resembled champion flat-race jockey Steve Donoghue, Bobby could be frustrating at times, especially when in possession. He had the tendency to hold on to the ball for too long and many attacks broke down because of his supposed greediness. Nevertheless, he could be a handful for any defender and, when in full flight, he certainly got the fans cheering.

He was an ever-present player in his first season with Stoke (scoring 10 goals) but was injured on the opening day of the 1926–27 campaign, against Bradford Park Avenue. Consequently, he missed the next 26 League and Cup games before returning to the team in the inside-left position with Dick Johnson, his wing partner. From that moment on, until the end of the season, the pair played superbly well together as Stoke roared on to clinch the Third Division North title. Bobby himself claimed six goals and had a helping hand in five others, including the winners against Crewe Alexandra, Durham and Accrington Stanley.

In 1927–28 he was switched back to his favourite position on the left wing and was absent just once (against Fulham at home) as the Potters consolidated themselves in the Second Division. In fact, over a period of four seasons (1927 to 1931), he missed only six senior games (out of a possible 177) and scored 23 goals. He then played in the first 21 League encounters of 1931–32 before suffering a nasty knee injury, which, annoyingly for Bobby, dragged on far too long.

He eventually left the Potteries for Oakwell on a free transfer in May 1932. Unfortunately, he continued to struggle with injury while at the Yorkshire club and managed only six more League appearances (netting one goal) before announcing his retirement in May 1937. He returned to Glasgow to become an insurance agent, later taking up a casual scouting appointment with Bradford City, which enabled him to attend several matches in Scotland.

During World War One, Bobby was an active soldier in the army, serving his country in France, Belgium, Denmark, Italy and South America. He played regularly for his unit, making over 100 appearances and scoring 20 goals. He came mighty close to gaining a Victory International cap for Scotland against Ireland in Belfast in 1919, but in the end he missed out as Jocky McPhail (Kilmarnock) was chosen instead. In 1920 he was named as reserve to the great Glasgow Rangers winger Alan Morton for the Home Internationals.

Bobby was 71 years of age when he died after a short illness early in 1966. He had a footballing brother, John, who kept goal for Albion Rovers, Chelsea, Reading, Newcastle United, Grimsby Town and Darlington.

Len Armitage

Born: 20 October 1899, Sheffield, Yorkshire
Died: 12 May 1972, Wortley, near Sheffield

Stoke City record:
Appearances: League 194, FA Cup 6
Goals: League 19
Debut: League, 15 March 1924 v Bury (a) lost 1–0

Also played for: Sheffield Forge and Rolling Mills FC, Walkley Amateurs, Wadsley Bridge, Sheffield Wednesday, Leeds United, Wigan Borough, Rhyl, Port Vale

At Schoolboy level, Yorkshireman Len Armitage was regarded as a 'terrific talent' who could, and would, play anywhere just to get a game of football. After gaining a winners' medal with Sheffield in the Final of the English Schools Shield in 1914, several top-class managers sought his signature.

In the end he chose to join his home-town club, Sheffield Wednesday, signing initially as an amateur in October 1914 before turning professional in August 1919, having served as a soldier during World War One. Just under a year later, in May 1920, he became one of the first players to sign for the restructured Leeds United side, scoring the first-ever League goal for the Elland Road club against South Shields on 1 September 1920, and going on to net 14 times in 53 games.

Following a 12-month spell with Wigan Borough, when he weighed in with another 21 goals in only 28 League starts, he moved to Stoke in an exchange deal involving Andy Smith in March 1924 and turned out in just three matches for them that term.

Originally an out-and-out centre-forward, Len was as 'strong as a bull' and utterly fearless. He had a tremendous 'engine', and was able to cover acres of ground during every game he played in. He helped the Potters win the Third Division North title in 1926–27 and represented the FA XI against South Africa two years later.

In his first full season at the Victoria Ground (1924–25), Len shared the centre-forward berth with 'Arty' Watkin and later with Dick Johnson, scoring twice (his first goal earning a 1–0 win at Leicester) in 18 senior outings. The following season he made only 14 League starts when occupying the outside-right, inside-right and centre-forward positions as the Potters battled hard and long, without success, to avoid relegation from the Second Division. In fact, Len suffered his fair share of injuries and twice left the field during matches. He was one of six players who lined up on the right wing and one of four who were selected to lead the Stoke attack.

In 1926–27, due to injury and illness, Len appeared in only three League games (all won) in place of John Beswick at centre-half, having been asked to fill in during an emergency. He was then switched to the right-half berth for the start of the 1927–28 campaign and played in 38 games that season, helping Stoke consolidate themselves back in the Second Division.

Injuries apart, he continued to perform well throughout the next three seasons before losing his place in the side to the former Ayr United player Bill Robertson, early in 1931–32. He had only four outings in his last season, with his 200th and final appearance coming against Southampton (at home) in January 1932, when he set up one of his side's goals in a 2–0 win.

At the end of that season, having struck 19 goals in exactly 200 first-team appearances for Stoke, Len left the Victoria Ground for non-League Rhyl, but within a matter of four months he had moved back to Stoke-on-Trent to sign for City's arch rivals, Port Vale, in December 1932. He continued to play as a defender but lost his place due to a knee injury in March 1933, and as a result he left the Valiants in May 1934, retiring shortly afterwards.

The grandson of a Yorkshire cricketer, Len continued to support both Stoke City and Port Vale and also attended League games at Hillsborough for many years until his death in 1972 at the age of 72.

Bill Asprey

Born: 11 September 1936, Wolverhampton

Stoke City record:
Appearances: League 304, FA Cup 19, League Cup 18
Goals: League 23, FA Cup 2, League Cup 1
Debut: League, 20 March 1954 v Oldham Athletic (h) lost 1–0

Also played for: Oldham Athletic, Port Vale
Managed: Oxford United, Stoke City

Bill Asprey was signed on amateur forms by Stoke City manager Frank Taylor in May 1953 from under the nose of his Wolverhampton Wanderers counterpart Stan Cullis.

As a youngster Bill had watched both Cullis and Taylor play for Wolves and would have loved to join the Molineux club. However, it was not to be and, as a 'Potter', he developed quickly at the Victoria Ground. After establishing himself in the first team during the 1957–58 season, he went from strength to strength, performing superbly at full-back (his preferred position) and occasionally as a central-defender or striker.

Bill went on to appear in 341 senior games for Stoke, scoring 26 goals. He helped them win the Second Division Championship in 1962–63 and reach the League Cup Final the following year. On leaving the Victoria Ground, he joined Oldham Athletic for £19,000 and after a brief spell with Port Vale took up coaching, first with Sheffield Wednesday (from February 1969) and then with Coventry (from February 1970), as well as having spells with Wolves and West Bromwich Albion. He later served in Rhodesia (from May 1975 until January 1978), where he was director of football, and coached in the Middle East (February–April 1978).

In July 1979 he took over as manager of Oxford United, retaining his position until December 1980 when he became coach to the Syrian national team, only to return to the Victoria Ground as assistant manager to Richie Barker, in February 1982.

In December 1983 he replaced Barker in the 'hot seat', but in May 1985 he was sacked after the Potters finished bottom of the First Division with only 17 points out of a possible 126. He was replaced by Mick Mills.

Going back to his playing days, Bill made his debut in 1954 but had to wait until April 1956 for his second Stoke game. The following term he added a further nine appearances to his tally before gaining a regular place in the side in 1957–58, when his fellow half-backs were Ken Thomson and Johnny Sellars. He had 28 outings that term and also netted his first Stoke League goal, sadly to no avail, as the Potters lost 5–3 at Bristol Rovers.

An ever present in 1958–59, he missed six matches the following season and nine in 1960–61, when he occupied five positions – right-back, right-half, centre-half, inside-right and inside-left. He netted seven goals as an emergency striker, including a hat-trick in a 5–3 home win over Charlton and a brace in a 9–0 hammering of Plymouth.

An ever present again in 1961–62, when he played at full-back with Tony Allen, Bill was outstanding in 1962–63 when once more he played in every game and helped the Potters win the Second Division title, netting five more goals, including two in a 3–3 draw with Derby County.

Playing behind ex-Wolves star Eddie Clamp and former England winger Stanley Matthews, he produced some terrific performances as Stoke pipped Chelsea to the title by a single point (53–52). The crunch match came at Stamford Bridge on 11 May. With only three games to follow, Stoke knew that a win would put them in the driving seat. They gained a 1–0 victory courtesy of Jimmy McIlroy's fine goal in front of a massive 66,199 crowd – the biggest audience any Stoke team had played in front of since 1946.

The following term, Bill played in the League Cup Final – the first major Final in Stoke's history. Unfortunately, Leicester City took the prize over two legs.

At this juncture, Bill was playing well and continued to impress in 1964–65, making his 300th League appearance, against Leeds United at Elland Road in April. However, the following season he was replaced at right-back by Eric Skeels and subsequently moved to Oldham, for whom he made 80 appearances in the Third Division before ending his career with 32 outings for Port Vale. He retired in December 1968 with 453 appearances under his belt.

As Stoke's manager, Bill saw the team win only 14 of 67 League games - but as a player, he was without doubt one of the best defenders Stoke City produced during the 1950s.

In later life, Bill ran a hotel on the south coast.

George Baddeley

Born:	8 May 1874, Fegg Hayes, Stoke-on-Trent
Died:	18 July 1952, West Bromwich

Stoke City record:

Appearances:	League 208, FA Cup 17
Goals:	League 14, FA Cup 5
Debut:	League, 2 September 1901 v Bury (h) lost 2–1

Also played for: Fegg Hayes Youth Club, Pitshill, Biddulph, West Bromwich Albion

One of four footballing brothers, George Baddeley was a splendid wing-half, confident on the ball, powerful in the tackle, strong in the air and very energetic. He began playing competitively with one of his local clubs, Pitshill, and after that assisted Biddulph. He was 26 years of age when he joined Stoke as a full-time professional in May 1900. Once he had bedded himself into the side, George proved to be a very consistent performer and was a first-team regular from September 1903 until May 1908, when the Potters lost their Football League status.

During his time at the Victoria Ground, George captained the team for long periods and scored a total of 19 goals in 225 League and Cup appearances. Deputising for Billy Leech, he made seven appearances in his first full season of senior football (1901–02) and followed up by making 33 in 1902–03 and scoring three goals, his first earning a point from a 1–1 draw with Sunderland in November. He also netted his first FA Cup goal in a 2–0 second-round replay victory at Nottingham Forest.

Thereafter, George was the mainstay of Stoke's defence, making 35, 36, 36, 35 and 43 appearances respectively over the next five seasons, being an ever present on two occasions and having one unbeaten run of 105 consecutive games between 14 February 1903 and 26 December 1905. His best scoring campaign came in 1907–08 when he bagged five goals, including a brilliant long-range effort in a 6–0 home League win over Fulham, the decider in a 1–0 away victory over Leeds City and another fine strike in a 4–2 triumph at Chesterfield. On checking the reference books and newspapers, it seems that all but two of George's 19 goals for Stoke were scored from outside the penalty area.

George made his 200th League appearance for the club against Bradford City at Valley Parade on 21 March 1908, but it was a game he quickly wanted to forget as the Potters crashed to a 6–0 defeat.

George moved to West Bromwich Albion for £250 in May 1908. He replaced Sammy Timmins at right-half in the Albion side and went on to spend six seasons at The Hawthorns, playing in front of the legendary English international full-back Jesse Pennington, as well as lining up with ex-Stoke players Ross Fielding, Fred Brown and Fred Rouse.

He made more than 150 senior outings for the Baggies and scored only one goal, in a 2–0 win away to Glossop North End in December 1910. He gained a Second Division Championship-winners' medal in 1910–11 and an FA Cup runners'-up medal the following year, when Albion lost 1–0 in a replay to Barnsley.

George still holds the record of being the oldest player ever to appear in a Football League game for West Bromwich Albion. He was almost 40 years old when he lined up against Sheffield Wednesday on 18 April 1914. He retired a month later after six years with the Black Country club. He remained in the town and attended games at The Hawthorns whenever possible. He was also a guest of the club when the First Division Championship was won in 1920 and, 11 years later, he was invited to Wembley when Albion completed the first half of their unique double by beating Birmingham in the Cup Final. George was a publican in West Bromwich at the time, acting as mine host of the Crown & Cushion.

Sam Baddeley

Born:	12 July 1884, Norton in the Moors, Staffordshire
Died:	Autumn 1960, Stoke-on-Trent

Stoke City record:

Appearances:	League 1, FA Cup 14, others 188
Goals:	Others 9
Debut:	League, 8 February 1908, Stockport County (h) won 1–0
Also played for:	Ball Green, Endon, Burslem Port Vale, Kidsgrove Wellington (Stoke-on-Trent)

Another member of the famous Baddeley footballing family, Sam was a strong-tackling, highly competitive defender who could occupy, with authority and grim determination, all three half-back positions. He was 23 years of age when he joined Stoke in the summer of 1907, shortly after his previous club, Burslem Port Vale, had hit financial difficulties which subsequently led to the club's liquidation.

Sam started out as an amateur utility forward, scoring plenty of goals for three local clubs – Ball Green (with whom he had two spells), Endon and Norton – before signing for Port Vale as a full-time professional in October 1905. He was successfully converted into a centre-half by the Valiants, for whom he played for almost two seasons up to his move across the Potteries to the Victoria Ground.

Sam made his senior debut for the Vale in a Second Division encounter against Leicester Fosse in September 1906, and went on to appear in 34 League and FA Cup games for the club before making an impact with the Potters.

A very consistent player, he always wanted to be involved in the action, whether it be defending or driving forward to assist his front men. He scored nine goals in 203 first-team appearances for Stoke. In May 1915 he left to join Kidsgrove Wellington, with whom he played throughout World War One, although he did not reappear when League football resumed in 1919.

He was a key member of Stoke's Southern League (Western) Division Two Championship-winning side in 1909–10, missing only one game, and he appeared in 56 first-team matches the following season, scoring the winning goal in a Birmingham League victory over Crewe Alexandra in December 1910 and netting a decisive one in a 3–2 win over Wolverhampton Wanderers reserves at Molineux on April Fool's Day.

He was partnered in the Stoke half-back line by several fine players including Bill Bradbury, Ellis Hall, Welsh international Joey Jones, Harry Leese and occasionally by Charlie Palmer. One feels that if Stoke had been members of the Football League around this time then their middle trio with Sam outstanding, week in, week out, would have competed exceedingly well. They undoubtedly did compete well in a first-round FA Cup tie in January 1910 when they gave the subsequent winners of the trophy, Newcastle United, a serious run for their money before losing 2–1 in a replay. They also produced a fine display the following season before slipping out of the competition to Manchester City.

Sam was brilliant against Newcastle and was bitterly disappointed to finish on the losing side, having manfully and doggedly helped stem the flow of several Geordie attacks with some brave and competent defending.

On his departure from the Victoria Ground, which effectively ended the link between the club and the Baddeley family, Sam played on until he was 35 years of age. He then worked briefly in the pottery business in Stoke-on-Trent and also tried his hand in the licensing trade. He remained in the Stoke area until his death in 1960.

There were four brothers in the Baddeley family, and they all played professionally for Stoke – George and Sam (who are both featured in this book) and Amos and Tom. The latter was a goalkeeper born in Bycars, Stoke-on-Trent, who also played for Bradford Park Avenue, Port Vale and Wolves. He won five England caps but only managed eight outings for the Potters during season 1910–11. Amos scored 56 goals in 101 appearances for Stoke between 1906 and 1912. He also played for Blackpool and Walsall, and later managed Abertillery and Ebbw Vale. There was a Baddeley on Stoke's books for 15 years (1900–15), and between them they amassed a combined total of 537 first-team games for the Potters.

Frank Baker

Born:	22 October 1918, Stoke-on-Trent
Died:	13 December 1989, Stoke-on-Trent

Stoke City record:

Appearances:	League 161, FA Cup 13, wartime 17
Goals:	League 32, FA Cup 1, wartime 1
Debut:	League, 26 December 1936 v Liverpool (h) drew 1–1

Also played for: Burslem Port Vale, Stafford Rangers, Leek Town

Stoke City manager Bob McGrory pipped Wolves boss Major Frank Buckley for Frank Baker's signature in June 1936. The Stoke-born outside-right, who had driven a laundry van while playing as an amateur with Port Vale in their Cheshire League team, went on to give the Potters excellent service over the next 13 years or so, appearing in 174 League and Cup games and scoring 33 goals either side of World War Two as well as having 17 outings during the hostilities.

Able to occupy both wing positions, Frank failed to make Vale's senior team and had to wait until Boxing Day 1936 before enjoying his first taste of League football, deputising for Joe Johnson on the left wing against Liverpool in front of almost 39,000 spectators at the Victoria Ground. He played well, came close to scoring and was retained for the next game away at Chelsea.

Johnson, however, remained first choice but when he was injured in the opening game of the 1937–38 season (against Birmingham), Frank went straight into the team. He produced some excellent performances and scored some cracking goals, including two in a 5–1 Christmas Day League victory over Grimsby Town. He held his position through to the end of the campaign, seeing the aforementioned Johnson transferred to West Bromwich Albion in between times.

The following season Frank missed just six League matches and netted another 10 goals, including a fine winner at Birmingham (2–1) and a wonderful effort in a 6–1 home victory over Chelsea.

Unfortunately, the outbreak of World War Two curtailed competitive League and Cup football until the 1945–46 season, by which time Frank was 27 years old and had also needed to recover from a broken leg. He was soon back in the thick of the action and made 11 appearances in that transitional campaign. Frank was in the Stoke side against Bolton in a sixth-round FA Cup replay at Burnden Park when 33 spectators were killed and over 500 injured after crush barriers had collapsed on a section of terracing.

Frank, and others who were present, never forgot that incident and some years later he recalled the moment the game was stopped and the players hovered around in groups in the centre circle. It was not until after the final whistle had sounded and the players had reached the dressing rooms that the players themselves were given the news of the tragedy. Some, including Frank, broke down in tears.

Frank was switched to the inside-left position on the commencement of the 1946–47 season to accommodate Alex Ormston, but still scored six goals in 44 outings. Sadly, in August 1947, in a home game against Liverpool, he broke his leg for a second time and was sidelined for almost six months. Nevertheless, he returned full of vim and vigour and scored three times in 11 appearances during the second half of the season, helping the Potters pull clear of the relegation zone.

Having played very well during the opening two and a half months of season 1948–49, Frank was again hindered when he suffered yet another fracture of his left leg, playing against the reigning FA Cup holders Manchester United. This time he was sidelined for five months, making his return against United at Old Trafford in mid-March.

A fighter to the last, Frank continued to play, and play well, for the Potters but amazingly he suffered a fourth broken leg, against Manchester City in October 1949, and this time he failed to make a full recovery.

He remained a registered player with Stoke until May 1951, when he left the Victoria Ground to sign for Stafford Rangers, later assisting Leek Town before retiring at the age of 34 in May 1953.

On leaving football, Frank became a fish and chip shop proprietor in Fenton. He was 71 when he died in 1989.

Gordon Banks, OBE

Born: 30 December 1937, Tinsley, Sheffield

Stoke City record:
Appearances: League 194, FA Cup 27, League Cup 19, others 6
Debut: League, 22 April 1967 v Chelsea (a) lost 1–0

Also played for: Millspaugh Steelworks, Rawmarsh Welfare, Chesterfield, Leicester City, Fort Lauderdale Strikers, Cleveland Stokers, NASL All Stars, England (2 Under-23 and 73 full caps)
Managed: Telford United

Gordon Banks was by far the finest goalkeeper in the world during the period from 1968 to 1971. Some people in football even class him as being the greatest 'keeper of all time, and that tremendous save from Pelé's downward header in the 1970 World Cup Finals in Mexico is rated the greatest save ever made in top-class football. It is still, to this day, regularly shown on TV in countries all over the world and also on virtually every goalkeeping coaching course.

At the time, Gordon was a Stoke City player, having joined the club as a 29-year-old in the summer of 1967 from Leicester City for what was to prove a bargain fee of £52,000. He made his Potters debut at Chelsea and was, in fact, the fourth goalkeeper used that season by Stoke manager Tony Waddington. He retained his place in the side, unchallenged for five years, until eventually being replaced by John Farmer, his understudy during that period.

A Yorkshireman, Gordon played his early football with Millspaugh Steelworks FC (two spells) and Rawmarsh Welfare. In the summer of 1954 he signed amateur forms for Chesterfield and turned professional at Saltergate in September 1955. He went on to appear in just 23 League games for the Spireites and gained an FA Youth Cup runners'-up medal before transferring to Filbert Street in May 1959 for a moderate fee of £7,000.

At Leicester he added a further 293 League and 63 Cup outings to his tally, including one against his future club, Stoke City, in the 1964 League Cup Final. He also played in two losing FA Cup Final sides, versus Spurs in 1961 and against Manchester United two years later. He won the first of his 73 full England caps in April 1963 (against Scotland), having already played twice for the Under-23 side. He later represented the Football League on six occasions.

A year before moving to the Victoria Ground, Gordon gained a World Cup-winners' medal, helping England defeat West Germany 4–2 after extra-time at Wembley. His haul of caps when he switched from Filbert Street to the Potteries stood at 37 – making him Leicester's most capped player at that time (his record was later beaten by the Northern Ireland defender John O'Neill, who had amassed a total of 39).

Gordon added 36 more caps to his collection with the Potters, and he remains to this day Stoke's most capped player at full international level.

Awarded the OBE in 1970 (after his World Cup heroics), Gordon appeared in a total of 246 senior games

for Stoke, gaining a League Cup-winners' tankard in 1972 (against Chelsea). He was additionally named both Footballer of the Year and Sportsman of the Year. In 1977 he was voted the NASL Goalkeeper of the Year when serving with Fort Lauderdale Strikers – five years after he had been involved in a horrific car smash which cost him the sight in his right eye and forced him into an early retirement from League football in this country. The accident took place five miles from Ashley Heath on 22 October 1972 when his Ford Granada crashed head-on with an Austin van.

When Fort Lauderdale lured him over to America, Banks' first thoughts were that he was joining a circus act, and he admitted to seeing billboards reading 'Roll-up, roll-up – come and see the greatest one-eyed goalkeeper in the world!'

An immensely likeable man, Gordon coached at the Victoria Ground after retiring and he also assisted on the coaching staff at Vale Park before becoming general manager of Telford United. He later ran his own sports promotion agency and is now president of Stoke City Football Club.

Mike Bernard

Born: 10 January 1948, Shrewsbury

Stoke City record:
Appearances: League 124+10, FA Cup 22, League Cup 15, others 6
Goals: League 6, FA Cup 2, League Cup 2, others 1
Debut: League, 16 April 1966 v Liverpool (a) lost 2–0

Also played for: Everton, Oldham Athletic, England (3 Under-23 caps)

Mike Bernard was a hard-tackling, resourceful wing-half who, if required, could also play at full-back. He accumulated a fine record during his six years in Stoke City's first team, appearing in 177 League and Cup games and scoring 11 goals. He was also capped three times by England at Under-23 level, lining up against West Germany, Sweden and Wales in the 1970–71 season.

He joined the playing staff at the Victoria Ground as a teenager in April 1964 and turned professional two years later. After biding his time in the reserves, Mike was handed his League debut by manager Tony Waddington in April 1966, when he partnered Dennis Viollet and Calvin Palmer in midfield against the reigning FA Cup holders Liverpool, in front of more than 41,000 spectators at Anfield. The Potters lost 2–0, but Mike played well enough and appeared in two more matches at the end of that season, scoring his first goal for the club in a 3–1 home victory over Wembley-bound Sheffield Wednesday. He was given only five outings in 1966–67 and a further 18 (five as a substitute) the following season before becoming a regular in the side halfway through the 1968–69 campaign.

At this juncture Stoke were a middle-of-the-table First Division team who occasionally pulled off a shock result and Mike was in the thick of the action, competing earnestly and vigorously week after week. Unfortunately, he was pegged back by injury in 1969–70 (making only 11 appearances) but he stormed back in 1970–71 and helped the Potters reach the semi-finals of the FA Cup with some sterling displays, especially in the sixth-round win at Hull and in the first semi-final encounter against Arsenal, which ended in a 2–2 draw. The Gunners won the replay and a disappointed Mike commented afterwards 'We (the players) were shell-shocked in the dressing room...we deserved to win that game – we were by far the better side.'

Twelve months on, it was a totally different story as Stoke again reached the semi-final stage of the FA Cup, as well as playing at Wembley, beating Chelsea 2–1 to win the League Cup.

In the latter competition, Mike had scored a fine goal in a 4–1 fifth-round win at Bristol Rovers and he stepped up with another, which was perhaps more important, in the 3–2 semi-final second replay victory over West Ham United. He then worked extremely hard at Wembley and duly celebrated victory with his colleagues as Stoke lifted the first major trophy in the club's history.

Unfortunately, six weeks after that superb win, the Potters crashed out of the FA Cup again, beaten for the second time running by Arsenal.

Almost immediately after that defeat, Mike was transferred to Everton for £140,000. He linked up with Colin Harvey and former 'Potter' Howard Kendall in the Merseysiders' midfield and played in the 1977 League Cup Final defeat to Aston Villa. After five years and more than 170 appearances, Mike left Goodison Park for Oldham Athletic in July 1977. He served the Latics for two years before announcing his retirement from competitive football in May 1979.

He became a Dee Valley publican in Chester but later returned to the game as football in the community officer at Crewe Alexandra, later working on the commercial side at Gresty Road.

As time went by, he switched localities and went to live and work in Swindon, where he dabbled in repairing lawnmowers and general maintenance work as a gardener. He now earns a living as a painter and decorator, while keeping in touch with his former teammates at Stoke City via the ex-players' association.

George Berry

Born:	19 November 1957, Rostrop, West Germany

Stoke City record:

Appearances:	League 229+8, FA Cup 15, League Cup 10, others 7
Goals:	League 27, FA Cup 1, others 2
Debut:	League, 28 August 1982 v Arsenal (h) won 2–1
Also played for:	Wolverhampton Wanderers, Doncaster Rovers, Peterborough United, Preston North End, Aldershot, Stafford Rangers, Wales (5 full caps)

George Berry, loose-limbed with a deceptively casual style, was a strong-tackling, determined and wholehearted central-defender who became a firm favourite with the fans at the Victoria Ground following his transfer from Wolves in 1982.

Born in Germany to a Jamaican father and a Welsh mother who originated from Mountain Ash, Glamorgan, he came over to England as a youngster and initially attended school in Blackpool and later in Handsworth (Birmingham) where he was always wanting to get involved in playground kick-abouts as well as joining other lads down at the local park.

He had an unsuccessful trial with Ipswich Town before joining Wolves as an apprentice in April 1974, turning professional on his 18th birthday. He made his League debut against Chelsea in the penultimate game of the 1976–77 season, when both clubs were fighting fiercely for the Second Division title, which Wolves eventually won.

Three years later, George gained a League Cup-winners' medal when Nottingham Forest were defeated 1–0 in the Final at Wembley. He proceeded to play in 160 senior games for the Molineux club, scoring six goals. He also won four full caps for Wales as a Wolves player, the first coming ironically against the country of his birth, West Germany, in a European Championship qualifier at Wrexham in May 1979. He was also only the second black player (after Ted Paris) to represent the principality. Unfortunately for George, Wales lost 2–0. His other international appearances came against the Republic of Ireland, West Germany (again) and Turkey in 1979–80, and his fifth and final game was against England in 1982–83, as a Stoke player.

Injuries and suspension affected George's performances during his last two years with Wolves and, after a very uneasy 1981–82 campaign which ended in relegation, he was transferred to Stoke City, where he was reunited with his former teammate Derek Parkin and manager Sammy Chung.

Scoring on his debut against Arsenal, George quickly bedded in at the heart of the Potters' defence, forming a terrific central partnership with England international Dave Watson. He made 34 appearances and netted five goals in his first season at the Victoria Ground but injuries meant that he managed only nine games in 1983–84. He regained full fitness the following season and played in 32 competitive matches, making 48 appearances in 1985–86, 46 in both the 1986–87 and 1987–88 campaigns and 37 in 1988–89, when once again he was plagued by niggling injuries.

Not getting any younger and with Ian Cranson and Chris Kamara effectively the first-choice centre-backs, George became surplus to requirements following the arrival of Noel Blake. After appearing in 260 first-class matches for the Potters in eight years, some as captain, and scoring 30 goals (a third of them from the penalty spot), he moved down the League ladder to Peterborough United in July 1990, switching to Preston North End a year later. However, he did not enjoy playing on Deepdale's plastic pitch and, due to a tedious knee problem, he was loaned out to Aldershot before drifting into non-League football with Stafford Rangers in August 1992, later becoming commercial manager when the club were members of the GM Vauxhall Conference.

In 1996 George was appointed on a full-time basis by the PFA, working alongside chief executive Gordon Taylor, Pat Nevin and Brendon Batson. In 1998 he took a position with PFA Enterprises Ltd at its Manchester branch and later had his own programme on BBC Radio Stoke. George also contributed to the promotion of football at various schools, youth clubs and pre-arranged functions.

In the programme printed for his testimonial match in August 1990, former Wolves striker John Richards wrote '…Whether on the field or in the dressing room, George's infectious and audible enthusiasm was an example to any player young and old. A bit wearing on the eardrums, but he could not be faulted for his dedication and wholehearted commitment to the game.'

Wayne Biggins

Born:	20 November, 1961, Sheffield

Stoke City record:

Appearances:	League 150+11, FA Cup 6, League Cup 11+1, others 11+1
Goals:	League 56, League Cup 4, others 7
Debut:	League, 19 August 1989 v West Ham United (h) drew 1–1

Also played for:	Lincoln City, King's Lynn, Matlock Town, Burnley, Norwich City, Manchester City, Barnsley, Celtic, Luton Town, Wigan Athletic, Leek Town, Stocksbridge Park Steels (also manager)

A smart striker who was nicknamed 'Bertie' throughout his career, Wayne Biggins was a latecomer to League football, and although he began his professional career with Lincoln City (signing as an 18-year-old at Sincil Bank in 1979) he played only eight times for the Imps before being released. He then appeared in non-League football for three years with Matlock Town and then King's Lynn while working as a hod carrier, eventually finding his way back into top-line League action in February 1984 with Burnley, who signed him for £7,500.

Wayne scored 43 goals in 101 senior appearances for the Clarets, and this sort of form attracted the attention of several clubs, one being Norwich City, whose manager Ken Brown duly signed Wayne for £40,000 in October 1985. At the time the Canaries were in the process of re-building their squad following relegation from Division One and were looking to bounce back at the first attempt. They succeeded, and Wayne ended that season with a Championship medal to his name after netting seven important goals. He stayed at Carrow Road until the summer of 1988, having netted eight times in 33 starts. At that point, Manchester City's new boss Mel Machin, who had until that summer been Brown's assistant at Norwich, took Wayne to Maine Road for a fee of £150,000.

Wayne proceeded to score nine goals in 32 games for City before Lou Macari signed him for the Potters for £250,000 in August 1989. Sharp, decisive, with a good turn of foot and an eye for goal, Wayne did superbly well at the Victoria Ground. He became the idol of the fans at the Boothen End, and over the next three years or so produced some tremendous performances. Forming a fine partnership with first Tony Ellis and then Mark Stein, he found the net on a regular basis, top-scoring three seasons running and helping Stoke win the Autoglass Trophy at Wembley in 1992. He played one of his best games for the club that day, admitting that the 1–0 victory over Stockport County in front of more than 48,000 spectators was his 'best day in football'.

However, in October 1992 Wayne was sold to Barnsley for £200,000, and 13 months later he was re-signed by his former manager, Macari, who had taken over the hot-seat at Celtic. Unfortunately, Wayne's time with the famous Glasgow club coincided with a period generally regarded by the Bhoys' loyal fans as one of the worst in their history. After struggling to make an impact in the green and white hoops, and not being one of the supporters' favourite sons, Wayne returned to Stoke, having spent just four months north of the border and made only 10 first-class appearances (six as a substitute).

Second time round he remained a 'Potter' until July 1995, including a spell on loan with Luton Town early in 1995. He rounded off his League career by assisting Oxford United and then Wigan Athletic, helping the latter win the Third Division title.

In May 1997 Wayne drifted back into non-League soccer by signing for local Staffordshire club Leek Town and he eventually ended his playing days at Stocksbridge Park Steels, where he became assistant manager and later team manager, finally finishing his football career in May 2003, six months short of his 42nd birthday.

During his 15 years in first-class football, Wayne, who also played under manager John Deehan at three different clubs, scored over 150 goals in more than 500 appearances – a fine record for an exceptionally fine player.

Alan Bloor

Born: 16 March 1943, Longton, Stoke-on-Trent

Stoke City record:
Appearances: League 384+4, FA Cup 38, League Cup 37, others 11
Goals: League 17, League Cup 1, others 1
Debut: League, 18 September 1961 v Brighton and Hove Albion (h) lost
                 1–0

Also played for: Port Vale
Managed: Port Vale

Nicknamed 'Bluto', Alan Bloor was a local lad who certainly reached the top. At junior level he was one of the star defenders for Uttoxeter Road Primary and Queensbury Road Senior schools and he also represented Stoke-on-Trent schoolboys, going on to win England Youth caps and skippering his country at that level.

Born in the Potteries during World War Two, he signed professional forms with Stoke City on his 17th birthday but had to bide his time, as manager Tony Waddington was reluctant to introduce him to first-team action. Indeed, it was not until September 1961 that Alan finally entered League football, making his debut at centre-half alongside Eric Skeels in place of Ron Andrew in a 1–0 home defeat by Brighton.

He kept his place for the next two games and played in four more matches that season, including a devastating 5–1 defeat at Southampton. Derek Reeves, the player Alan was marking, netted twice and had a hand in two other goals.

It would be another three years before Alan finally established himself in Stoke City's first XI, and from then on he never looked back. He went from strength to strength and over a period of 12 years, playing mainly as partner to Denis Smith at the heart of the Potters' defence, he was an inspiring figure in the red-and-white striped shirt.

After having just a single outing in each of the 1962–63 and 1963–64 campaigns, he played in 21 fixtures in 1964–65 and scored his first goal to earn his team a point against the champions-elect, Manchester United, in front of more than 50,000 fans at Old Trafford. Two more goals followed for Alan in 1965–66 in home League victories over Fulham (3–2) and Sheffield United (2–0), and in 1967–68 he claimed four, including a cracker in a 4–3 win at Wolves.

At this juncture Alan had former England international left-back Tony Allen playing alongside him at the centre of the back four and, in 1968–69, he had no fewer than five different central defensive partners. One of them was Denis Smith, whom he would play alongside until 1974–75 when Alan Dodd, was cemented into the team by manager George Eastham.

In season 1971–72, Alan was outstanding as Stoke reached the Final of the League Cup after wins over Southport, Oxford United, Manchester United, Bristol Rovers and West Ham United. At Wembley, Alan had a terrific game when the team took on and beat Chelsea 2–1 to lift the first major trophy in the club's history.

This same season, and in the one before, he was a member of Stoke's beaten FA Cup semi-final team against Arsenal, and in 1973 he helped the Potters win the Watney Cup (against Hull City), having earlier tasted European football for the first time against the German side Kaiserslautern in the UEFA Cup.

After making just six League appearances for the Valiants, Alan retired to concentrate on coaching and in August 1979 was appointed caretaker manager at Vale Park, taking charge of the team on a full-time basis a month later. Unfortunately, he did not like the job, explaining 'I don't have what it takes', and resigned before the end of the year, handing over his duties to John McGrath.

After leaving football, Alan ran a successful carpet business in his native Longton.

Steve Bould

Born: 16 November 1962, Stoke-on-Trent

Stoke City record:

Appearances: League 179+4, FA Cup 10, League Cup 13, others 5
Goals: League 6, League Cup 1
Debut: League, 26 September 1981 v Middlesbrough (a) lost 3–2

Also played for: Torquay United, Arsenal, Sunderland, England (1 B and 2 full
                  caps)

Steve Bould signed for his hometown club, Stoke City, as a schoolboy in 1978 and turned professional in November 1980. He made his senior debut at right-back in a 3–2 defeat away to Middlesbrough in a First Division game in September 1981. However, he was unable to command a regular place in the team and was loaned out to Torquay United in October 1982, playing nine times for Bruce Rioch's side.

Steve slowly but surely began to show what a fine defender he was, and after some determined performances in the second team he eventually became a regular in the Potters first XI in 1983, taking over the number-two shirt from Derek Parkin. He played extremely well in season 1983–84 and also during the relegation campaign of 1984–85 before switching to the centre-half berth in March 1986, taking over the pivotal duties from Paul Dyson, who was transferred to West Bromwich Albion.

Partnering Welsh international George Berry at the heart of the Stoke City defence, Steve continued to produce some exquisite displays and, although the Potters struggled on the field, his performances were nothing less than inspired.

Unfortunately, a career-threatening back injury, suffered initially at Blackburn in March 1987, sidelined him for around seven months but, after a series of operations (including a major one), he battled back to full fitness. Steve took his tally of senior appearances for the Potters past the 200 mark before he left the Victoria Ground to sign for Arsenal for a tribunal-set fee of £390,000 in June 1988.

Replacing long-term hero David O'Leary at Highbury, Steve became part of Arsenal's 'famous four' defensive line up, with his former Stoke City teammate Lee Dixon, skipper Tony Adams and left-back Nigel Winterburn.

Steve helped the Gunners win the First Division title twice, in 1988–89 and 1990–91, when he was voted the supporters' Player of the Year, but he was bitterly disappointed when injury ruled him out of the FA Cup and League Cup Finals which Arsenal won in season 1992–93.

After collecting a European Cup-Winners' Cup Final medal in 1994 and missing the Final of the same competition the following season through suspension, success eluded Steve and Arsenal for several years, and the arrival of French manager Arsène Wenger led to some speculation that the ageing defender would leave the club, especially as he was now often second choice behind Martin Keown. Instead it only spurred Steve on to greater things and, as the Gunners got back to winning ways, Steve played a vital role in the team that won the Premiership and FA Cup double in 1997–98, when Steve famously set up Tony Adams with a chipped pass for the final goal in Arsenal's 4–0 win over Everton that clinched the title.

By now, age was not on Steve's side and, after a final season at Highbury when he took his appearance tally for the Gunners up to 372, he moved to Sunderland in July 1999 for a fee of £500,000. Manager Peter Reid immediately made him club captain. He stayed for two seasons at the Stadium of Light, but injury forced him to retire in September 2000, having played only 21 League games for Sunderland. He then began working towards his UEFA coaching badges and moved back to Arsenal in June 2001, becoming a coach for the youth teams.

Despite being part of one of the most secure top-flight defences of the late 1980s and early to mid-1990s, Steve won only two caps for England, far fewer than fellow centre-half Adams. His first was against Greece and his second versus Norway, both in 1994. He also played in one B international.

In the words of his former Arsenal teammate Tony Adams, 'Steve was a great competitor, cool, efficient, reliable and virtually unbeatable in the air.'

Frank Bowyer

Born:	10 April 1922, Chesterton, Stoke-on-Trent
Died:	11 November 1999, Torquay

Stoke City record:

Appearances:	League 398, FA Cup 38, wartime 162
Goals:	League 137, FA Cup 12, wartime 56
Debut:	Wartime, 20 January 1940 v Manchester United (a) lost 4–3
	League, 21 February 1948 v Manchester United (h) lost 2–0

Also played for: Macclesfield Town

Inside-forward Frank Bowyer joined Stoke City as an amateur in June 1937, soon after leaving Birches Head School. He developed quickly at Victoria Ground and turned professional in the summer of 1939. Unfortunately, World War Two disrupted his career at the outset and it was not until February 1948, when he was almost 26 years of age, that he finally played in the Football League for the first time, going on to make his FA Cup debut in January 1949 against Swindon Town.

Thankfully from Frank's point of view, and for the benefit of Stoke City, he was able to play football regularly during the hostilities (when he served in Palestine) and he did extremely well for the Potters, scoring 56 goals in 162 regional League and Cup matches, netting on his debut against Manchester United in 1940 and having his best season in 1942–43 when he struck 18 goals in 37 outings.

After the war he continued to work hard at his game and, on gaining a regular place in the first team (in 1948–49), he produced some superb displays over the next 12 years or so. Frank was being practically first choice at inside-forward, although injuries at times did knock him back somewhat, especially in 1951–52, when he appeared in only 19 competitive games.

Frank's best scoring season was his first – 1948–49 – when he cracked in 21 goals, including a wonderful hat-trick in a 3–1 win at Burnley. He had to wait until February 1955 before claiming his next treble, which came in a 4–2 home victory over Lincoln City. Frank formed exciting right-wing partnerships with several players, starting off with George Mountford, then Johnny Malkin, 'Tim' Coleman and finally Doug Newlands.

Frank continued to produce the goods for Stoke City until April 1960, when he quit the club after making 436 senior appearances and netting another 149 goals to become one of the finest marksmen in the club's history. He finished only 10 goals short of Freddie Steele's then record haul of 159 League and Cup goals for the club. In fact, Frank's overall record was very impressive – 598 first-team appearances (League, FA Cup, wartime) and 205 goals. Only three players – John McCue (675), Frank Mountford (608) and Eric Skeels (606) – have appeared in more first-team matches for the Potters and only two men to this day – Tommy Sale (282) and Steele – have scored more goals for Stoke City than Frank.

A quality player with an excellent shot (in both feet), Frank could also deliver an inch-perfect pass up to 40 yards, far better than the Fulham and England international Johnny Haynes could in his early days.

Frank went on the official FA tour to Canada in the summer of 1950, his only representative honour, although he was named twice on standby for the full England squad. Perhaps if he had been with a more fashionable club then he would have gained a full cap – he certainly deserved one.

Frank spent 23 years at the Victoria Ground and, on leaving the club, joined non-League side Macclesfield Town. He announced his retirement from the game in April 1962.

Jimmy Bradley

Born:	10 May 1881, Goldenhill, Stoke-on-Trent
Died:	12 March 1954, Blackpool

Stoke City record:

Appearances:	League 199, FA Cup 27, others 30
Goals:	League 4, others 2
Debut:	League, 3 September 1898 v Aston Villa (a) lost 3–1

Also played for: Goldenhill Wanderers, Liverpool, Reading

Wing-half Jimmy Bradley, a model of consistency with a terrific engine who tackled with great judgement and tenacity, scored six goals in a total of 256 League and Cup games for the club in two separate spells with Stoke, both before World War One.

Born in the Potteries in 1881, he signed for Stoke as a 16-year-old amateur from his local club Goldenhill Wanderers in February 1898, turning professional three months later. After a handful of second team outings, he made his senior debut in place of Arthur Rowley against Aston Villa in the second League match of the 1898–99 season. Rowley returned to the side at left-back and this allowed Jimmy to secure his place in the side on a permanent basis, seven weeks later. He remained a regular in the left-half position right up until September 1905 when he transferred to Liverpool, having turned down an offer to go to Southern League side Plymouth Argyle, saying 'Where's that? It seems miles away. I don't want to go there.'

A quality player, a great practical joker and the comedian in the dressing room, Jimmy had a favourite trick on the field of play whereby he would aim to kick the ball with his right foot but at the last possible moment would dummy his opponent and use the outside of his left leg to deliver an astute pass, clear his lines or even shoot at goal.

A defensive player rather than an attacking one, he netted only six goals for the Potters, having to wait until his 138th game before notching his first – a penalty in an emphatic 4–0 home League win over Sheffield Wednesday. He cracked home another spot kick in the next game against West Bromwich Albion (lost 2–1) and bagged two more League goals the following season, both at home, against Sheffield United (lost 4–3) and Sunderland (won 3–1). His other two goals came during his second spell with the club,

in Southern League matches against Luton Town (a) in April 1914 and Merthyr Town (h) in October 1914.

After the leaving the Victoria Ground for Anfield first time round in a £420 deal (a relatively generous sum in those days), Jimmy did very well on Merseyside. He gained a League Championship medal with Liverpool in 1905–06 when he made 31 appearances out of a possible 38 and represented the Football League against the Scottish League in 1906. He was desperately unlucky not to win a full England cap. In fact, he was on the brink of playing in his first senior international against Ireland in February 1907 but missed out to Robert Hawkes of Luton Town. He was later named reserve for his country twice.

Jimmy strove on manfully at Anfield, became a huge favourite with the supporters and was a terrific half-back partner to Alex Raisbeck. He scored eight goals in 184 competitive appearances for the Merseysiders before transferring to Reading in December 1910 for a small fee. He made over 100 appearances for the 'Biscuitmen', as they were then called, before returning to Stoke in August 1913; this, after having had his contract cancelled at Elm Park following an argument with fellow players and staff, which resulted in Jimmy throwing the whole of the Reading first team kit into the bath!

He continued to serve the Potters for another two seasons, eventually retiring in May 1915. He was appointed as a part-time coach (looking after the reserves) at the Victoria Ground, while also working for the Stoke-on-Trent Highways Department and occasionally turning out for his first club, Goldenhill Wanderers. Jimmy died in Blackpool at the age of 72.

His younger brother, Martin, an inside-forward, played for Grimsby Town (1907–08), Sheffield Wednesday (1910–11) and Bristol Rovers (1911–12).

Charlie Burgess

Born: 25 December 1883, Church Lawton, Staffordshire
Died: 11 December 1956, Hartshill, Stoke-on-Trent

Stoke City record:
Appearances: League 179, FA Cup 16
Debut: League, 1 February 1902 v Nottingham Forest (a) lost 2–0

Also played for: Talke Rangers, Butt Lane Swifts, Manchester City

Charlie Burgess was a cool and solid defender. Able to occupy both full-back positions but preferring the right, he was blessed with a crunching tackle, was never flustered and always played a calm, calculated game. A thinker with excellent positional sense, always ready to move into the middle to cover his centre-half, he could head a ball as well as anyone in the game and perhaps his only downfall was that he lacked speed when in a race for the ball with an opposing winger.

Charlie's father wanted him to become a farmer at the family's Field House Farm on Old Butt Lane, Church Lawton, and, in fact, young Charlie was employed in this role as a youngster. He also loved his football and played his early soccer with Talke Rangers and then Butt Lane Swifts before moving to Stoke as an amateur in March 1901. Charlie actually signed the appropriate forms while sitting on top of a haystack on his father's farm. He turned professional within a month and spent almost 12 months playing in the second team before making his debut in the Football League at right-back against Nottingham Forest in February 1902, deputising for the injured Sam Meredith, brother of the more famous Billy. He played in the next two games, away at Blackburn (lost 6–1) and against Small Heath (drew 1–1) before reverting to the reserves.

The following season, however, he gained a regular place in the first XI, taking over from Meredith and partnering Andy Clark as well as Harry Benson. He remained first choice, injuries permitting, until the Potters went bankrupt at the end of the 1907–08 season, a situation which certainly stunned Charlie and his teammates at the time.

During his last five years at the Victoria Ground, Charlie was also accompanied at full-back by regulars Arthur Hartshorne, Welsh international Lloyd Davies,

Ernie Mullineux and Billy Cope, in that order, and he produced some excellent displays, none more so than when champions-elect Sheffield Wednesday were thumped 4–0 at the Victoria Ground in November 1902 and Liverpool were beaten 2–1 on Boxing Day 1905.

Charlie was also outstanding during Stoke's successful battle to avoid relegation in 1903–04, when an unbeaten run of four matches right at the end of the campaign enabled them to retain their top flight status with a point to spare over demoted Liverpool and West Bromwich Albion.

A model of consistency, Charlie missed only six League games out of a possible 108 over a period of three seasons – 1905–08 – and it was surprising that he never scored a goal because he loved to get forward in support of his front men and, given the opportunity, produce a stinging right-foot shot.

Defending was Charlie's main objective and he did it splendidly for the Potters over seven years, skippering the team from time to time. He accumulated almost 200 competitive appearances before leaving the Victoria Ground for Manchester City (along with his Potters teammate Tom Holford) in the summer of 1908, when hard-up Stoke needed some ready cash!

He remained a registered player with City until April 1911, when he was forced to retire with the serious knee injury that had affected him since the start of the 1909–10 season (he went off injured in the opening League game against Blackpool). He never regained full fitness and made just 32 senior appearances for the Lancashire club, 26 of them coming in his first season when City were relegated to the Second Division. He later returned to the Potteries and worked in a factory for many years, attending Stoke home games whenever possible. Charlie was almost 73 years of age when he died.

John Butler

Born: 7 February 1962, Liverpool

Stoke City record:
Appearances: League 258+4, FA Cup 11, League Cup 19, others 26+1
Goals: League 7, others 2
Debut: League, 26 December 1988 v Manchester City (h) won 3–1

Also played for: Burscough, Prescot Cables, Wigan Athletic (2 spells)

A very commendable, consistent and reliable defender, John Butler was Stoke's regular right-back for most of his six and a half years at the Victoria Ground. Occasionally he was asked to play in other positions, mainly left-back, although he did wear the number-10 shirt for three games halfway through the 1993–94 season and again in his final year with the club.

A Liverpudlian, he assisted Merseyside clubs Burscough and Prescot Cables before becoming a full-time professional with Wigan Athletic in January 1982.

After more than 300 senior appearances for the Springfield Park club, whom he helped win promotion from the Fourth Division in his first season, he was transferred to the Potters for £75,000 in December 1988 and went straight into the side against Manchester City on Boxing Day, taking over from John Gidman and competing well in a 3–1 victory.

Lee Dixon had left the club in January 1988 and, for a good 11 months, the search went on for a suitable replacement while Stoke boss Mick Mills utilised several other players in the right-back position. However, John always seemed top of the wanted list and when the time was right he agreed to move south to the Potteries. What a tremendous signing he proved to be.

Retaining his position and becoming known as 'Mr Dependable', he went from strength to strength and produced some excellent performances, finally amassing a grand total of 319 League and Cup appearances and nine goals for the Potters.

He played his part in the 1–0 Autoglass Trophy Final win over Stockport County at Wembley in 1992 and, a year later, was a key member of Stoke's Second Division Championship-winning side. He appeared in 44 of the 46 scheduled League games, initially partnering the former West Bromwich Albion and England International Derek Statham and later lining up alongside Cliff Carr, plus a handful of other players who were asked to fill in at left-back by manager Lou Macari.

Strong in all departments of full-back play, John was also powerful in the air and was pretty quick over the ground as well, being able to match most wingers for pace in a chase down the line. He loved to overlap and was very useful at set pieces.

His goal tally was not brilliant but his effort proved vital when he did find the net. He hit the target in the 1–1 home draw with Tranmere Rovers in January 1991, scored the decider in a 2–1 home League victory over Bradford City three months later, weighed in with another fine effort in a 3–2 win over Hartlepool United in September 1991, struck the ball home in a 2–1 home triumph over Brentford in mid-January 1992 and bagged a crucial one in a 2–1 victory at Preston in October of that same year.

There was some speculation in the summer of 1992 that he might leave the club and join Coventry City but nothing materialised and John remained a 'Stokie' for another three years before choosing to return to his former club, Wigan Athletic, on a free transfer in June 1995. His place in the Potters' line up went to the versatile Ian Clarkson, who had arrived from Birmingham City in September 1993 and had already occupied a variety of defensive positions.

John continued to give a good account of himself with the Latics, gaining a Third Division Championship-winners' medal in his second year back before being released at the end of the 1996–97 season. His tally of senior appearances for his two major clubs was a creditable 687 (368 for Wigan), and he ended his career with 27 goals under his belt.

John is currently in the top six of Stoke City's champion full-back appearance-makers.

Mark Chamberlain

Born: 19 November 1961, Stoke-on-Trent

Stoke City record:

Appearances: League 110+2, FA Cup 4, League Cup 9
Goals: League 17, FA Cup 1
Debut: League, 28 August 1982 v Arsenal (h) won 2–1

Also played for: Port Vale, Sheffield Wednesday, Portsmouth, Brighton & Hove
                    Albion, Exeter City, Fareham Town (player-manager), England
                    (2 Schoolboy, 2 Youth, 4 Under-21 and 8 full caps)

Winger Mark Chamberlain scored 18 goals in 125 first-class appearances for the Potters, whom he served for three years. He joined Port Vale straight from school, signing as an apprentice in April 1977 and turning professional two years later. He switched to neighbours Stoke City for £135,000 in August 1982, was transferred to Sheffield Wednesday for £300,000 in September 1985, joined Portsmouth for £200,000 in August 1988, assisted Brighton & Hove Albion from August 1994 to August 1995 and starred for Exeter City until March 1997, when he became player-manager-coach of non-League side Fareham Town, later being engaged as director of football at that club from June 2000.

The younger brother of Neville, Mark spent 20 years in senior football, and made his League debut for Port Vale against Scunthorpe United in August 1978. He went on to appear in 110 competitive matches for the Valiants, scoring 20 goals and being named in the PFA team for 1981–82 before his switch across the city of Stoke to the Victoria Ground, goalkeeper Mark Harrison moving in the opposite direction.

A direct, fast-raiding winger, clever, with excellent ball control, he loved to take on defenders on the outside and could centre splendidly on the run and with great precision. He replaced Paul Maguire on Stoke's left wing at the start of the 1982–83 campaign and had an excellent first season with the club, scoring six times in 39 games as the Potters finished 13th in the top flight. Mark also had the pleasure of netting on his full international debut for England (under Bobby Robson) in a comprehensive 9–0 European Championship qualifying win over Luxembourg at Wembley in December. He went on to add a further seven caps to his tally as a 'Potter', the last in a 5–0 win over Finland in a World Cup qualifier in 1984. He had previously represented his country at Schoolboy, Youth and Under-21 levels.

In 1983–84, Chamberlain missed two League games as the Potters just managed to scramble clear of the relegation zone, but it all went wrong the following season as Stoke, who struggled from the first to the last game, went crashing through the trap-door and into the Second Division after securing only 17 points out of a possible 126 (three wins and eight draws). They finished rock bottom, 23 points adrift of 21st-placed Sunderland and with 73 fewer than champions Everton.

Chamberlain did his best but to no avail, and if the truth be known the team's horrid record was down to a terrible defence, which conceded 98 goals in total (91 in the League). The forwards were not much better, mustering only 24 goals in the League, Ian Painter top-scoring with six, of which four came from the penalty spot.

Sheffield Wednesday boss Howard Wilkinson, who had been looking for an out-and-out winger for quite a while, signed Chamberlain soon after the start of the 1985–86 season but he struggled with his form at Hillsborough and 24 of his 27 appearances for the Owls came as a substitute. He did not fare too well in 1986–87 or 1987–88, and when former Potters manager Alan Ball enquired about his availability he had no hesitation in signing for Portsmouth in readiness for the 1988–89 season. Unfortunately, he had a moderate first season at Fratton Park as Pompey struggled to retain their Second Division status, clinging on in 20th position after losing seven of the last eight League games

Things improved and in 1992 Chamberlain helped Portsmouth reach the semi-finals of the FA Cup, where they lost in a replay to Liverpool. Two years later he moved along the south coast to Brighton & Hove Albion on a free transfer, and the following season he teamed up with former Stoke teammate Peter Fox at struggling Exeter City. At the end of 1996–97, Chamberlain quit League football to become player-manager-coach and later director of football at Fareham Town.

Chamberlain's League career brought him 518 appearances and a total of 69 goals, a fine record for an out-and-out winger.

Lee Chapman

Born: 5 December 1959, Lincoln

Stoke City record:
Appearances: League 95+4, FA Cup 3, League Cup 5
Goals: League 34, FA Cup 1, League Cup 3
Debut: League Cup, 2 October 1979 v Swindon Town (a) lost 2–1

Also played for: Plymouth Argyle, Arsenal, Sunderland, Sheffield Wednesday, Champois Niortias (France), Nottingham Forest, Leeds United, Portsmouth, West Ham United, Southend United, Ipswich Town, Swansea City, Stafford Rangers, England (1 B and 1 Under-21 cap).

A nomadic 6ft 2in striker whose transfer fees amounted to almost £2.5 million, Lee Chapman served no fewer than 14 clubs over a period of 20 years, amassing 264 goals in almost 700 first-class appearances, including 197 goals in 552 Football League games. Not the most graceful of players, he was nevertheless strong in all aspects of forward play – courageous, willing, determined, brave and exceptionally dangerous in and around the penalty-area, especially with his head from set pieces.

Capped once by England at both B and Under-21 levels, Lee helped Nottingham Forest win both the 1989 League Cup and Simod Cup Finals, netting twice in the latter triumph over Everton at Wembley. He was also a member of Leeds United's Second and First Division Championship-winning sides of 1990 and 1992 respectively, and during his four years at Hillsborough he certainly gave the fans plenty to cheer about, netting some splendid goals with both head and feet.

Wherever he played, Lee certainly suffered his fair share of injuries but always came back for more. A battler to the end, he feared no one, gave as good as he got, and was a big favourite with the fans of every club he served – simply because he played to win.

Lee joined the playing staff of Stoke City, initially as an apprentice, in June 1976 and turned professional two years later when Alan Durban was his manager. Having hit the headlines as a junior with the Potters and once scoring six goals in an intermediate game, he spent a short period on loan with Plymouth Argyle (December 1978) before returning to the Victoria Ground and going on to net a debut goal for Stoke in a third-round League Cup defeat to Swindon. He became a first team regular halfway through the 1979–80 season, taking over from Brendan O'Callaghan as leader of the attack, and held his position, practically unchallenged, until the day he left.

Lee netted three League goals in his first season of senior football and followed up the next season with 15 in 41 League starts, plus two more in Cup competitions, finishing up on top of the scoring list. His latter haul included two hat-tricks, the first in a 3–1 home win over Norwich City and the second in a 3–1 victory over his future club Leeds United at Elland Road.

In 1981–82 Lee continued to trouble defenders and goalkeepers alike, netting a further 17 goals (16 in the League) and once again heading the club's scoring charts. Unfortunately for Stoke (and, indeed, the supporters), he left the Victoria Ground for Arsenal in a £500,000 transfer deal in August 1982, signed to replace John Hawley.

In December 1983 Lee switched his allegiance to Sunderland (signed for £200,000). He moved to Sheffield Wednesday for £100,000 in August 1984, had a spell in France with Chamois Niortais FC (June-October 1988), played for Nottingham Forest (recruited by Brian Clough for £350,000) and joined Leeds United for £400,000 in January 1990. He stayed at Elland Road for three and a half years before transferring south to Portsmouth for £250,000 in August 1993. He assisted West Ham United (briefly), had a loan spell with Southend United and starred for Ipswich Town before returning to Leeds, on loan, early in 1996, He finally ended his nomadic League career with Swansea City before having a farewell fling with Stafford Rangers, choosing to retire gracefully in 1997.

Married to former *Men Behaving Badly* actress Lesley Ash, Lee now runs a high-profile wine bar in Chelsea. His father, Roy Chapman, played for Aston Villa, Lincoln City, Mansfield Town, Port Vale and Chester, scoring over 200 goals in more than 400 games between 1953 and 1964. His mother, Margaret, was secretary to Stoke City manager Frank Taylor during the 1950s.

Tommy Clare

Born: 12 March 1865, Congleton, Cheshire
Died: 27 December 1929, Ladysmith, Vancouver, Canada

Stoke City record:
Appearances: League 221, FA Cup 29, others 1
Goals: League 4, FA Cup 2
Debut: FA Cup, 31 October 1885 v Crewe Alexandra (h) drew 2–2

Also played for: Talke Rangers, Goldenhill Wanderers, Burslem Port Vale (three
                 spells, one as a guest), Manchester City (trial), England (4 full
                 caps)

Full-back Tommy Clare was, according to the record books, the first player to sign as a full-time professional for Stoke, and he was also the club's first captain in the Football League, leading his side against the FA Cup holders West Bromwich Albion on the opening day of the newly formed competition on Saturday 8 September 1888.

An inspirational player, Tommy was a splendid header of the ball, quick off the mark, strong and purposeful in the tackle and ever-reliable, always working for his team. He cleared his lines very effectively, giving the ball one almighty kick downfield rather than just lifting it safely out of the danger zone.

Starting his senior career with Talke Rangers as a 15 year-old in 1880 and then assisting Goldenhill Wanderers (from August 1882), Tommy joined Burslem Port Vale in February 1884. Five months later, after only a handful of outings, he switched his allegiance to Stoke and made his senior debut in a Potters jersey that season, only to return to the Vale as a guest in November 1884. Returning to Stoke after just a week, Tommy bedded himself in and became a star performer in the right-back position, going on to amass over 250 League and Cup appearances for the club up to July 1897 when, perhaps surprisingly, he rejoined his former club, Burslem Port Vale, this time as player-coach.

As a 'Potter', Tommy represented Staffordshire in County fixtures on several occasions and gained four full England caps, lining up against Ireland in 1889 and 1892 (won 6–1 and 2–0 respectively), versus Wales in 1893 (won 6–0) and against Scotland in 1894 (drew 2–2). He played alongside two of his Stoke teammates, goalkeeper Billy Rowley and fellow full-back Alf Underwood, in the international against Ireland in 1892.

He missed only one League game in 1888–89, was absent from eight the following season, played as an ever-present in 1890–91, made 22 out of a possible 26 appearances in 1891–92 and was then virtually immovable, missing only eight games (five in 1894–95) out of a possible 150 during the next five seasons. He scored three of his six goals for the Potters in 1893–94, finding the net in both home and away games against Bolton Wanderers (a 4–1 away defeat and a 5–0 home victory). He also fired home a beauty against Newton Heath in a 3–1 triumph at the Victoria Ground.

When registered with the Valiants, Tommy played as a trialist in one League game for Manchester City against Newcastle United in March 1898, slotting in at left-back in a 2–0 defeat on Tyneside. After returning to the Vale he unfortunately broke his leg in October 1898 (against Grimsby Town), and although he regained full fitness he was never the same player again. In fact, he once turned out in goal for the Valiants against Gainsborough Trinity in March 1899, finishing on the losing side, 3–2.

He appeared in only 23 first-class matches for Vale and played in a total of 59 at all levels. He gained a Staffordshire Cup-winners' medal in 1898 when West Bromwich Albion were defeated 1–0 in the Final at his old hunting home, the Victoria Ground.

Retiring through injury at the end of the 1898–99 season, Tommy was persuaded to return to active duty the following year, alas without success. He was then out of football for five years, returning as player-secretary of Port Vale in July 1905. Unfortunately, with money tight, Vale could not afford to keep Tommy on their payroll beyond the next year and he left the club in April 1906.

He later went to live and work in Canada (emigrating shortly before World War One), where he remained until his death two days after Christmas 1929, at the age of 64.

Terry Conroy

Born: 2 October 1946, Dublin

Stoke City record:
Appearances: League 244+27, FA Cup 25, League Cup 23+3, others 10+1
Goals: League 49, FA Cup 8, League Cup 8, others 1
Debut: League, 6 September 1967 v Leicester City (h) won 3–2

Also played for: Glentoran, Bulova (Hong Kong), Crewe Alexandra, Republic of Ireland (26 caps)

Born Gerard but always referred to as Terry, Conroy was an immensely popular footballer from the day he joined Stoke City in a £10,000 transaction from Glentoran in March 1967 until the day he quit the club as a player in January 1980.

During the two years prior to Terry joining the Potters, there had seemingly been a club jinx on the number-seven shirt once worn by the great Stanley Matthews, who retired in 1965. In fact, no less than a dozen players had occupied the right-wing position, several of them without success. When Terry was handed the number-seven shirt early in the 1967–68 season, that jinx was laid to rest forever as the bonny red-haired Irishman retained it without any undue pressure, in the main, for the next 10 years or so as he accumulated well over 330 senior appearances for the club and scored 66 goals.

A scorer on his League debut against Leicester City in front of more than 19,000 fans at the Victoria Ground in September 1967, Terry made 11 competitive appearances that season but the following campaign he became a regular in the side, played in 36 games and scored nine goals. He starred in 33 more fixtures in 1969–70, netting just twice.

In 1970–71 and again in 1971–72, Terry was terrific, making almost 100 senior appearances in total and scoring 25 goals. He helped the Potters reach successive FA Cup semi-finals but each time they were defeated by Arsenal after a replay. Both defeats obviously upset Terry and his colleagues, but he and his teammates certainly made up for those huge disappointments by winning the League Cup at Wembley, beating the favourites Chelsea 2–1 with Terry scoring the first goal. He played exceedingly well in the Final, causing the usually sound and reliable Chelsea defence plenty of problems with his pace and trickery. The official video, released after that triumph, featured Terry giving a tremendous rendition of *We'll Be With You* while lying in a steamy bath.

In 1972–73 Terry was again in pretty good form, notching five goals in 39 outings, but the following season he struggled with injuries and only played in 11 matches, following up with 21 and 18 over the next two seasons. He was back to his best in 1976–77 (six goals in 38 games) but unfortunately his efforts could not prevent the Potters from slipping out of the top flight.

He did his best in 1977–78 (appearing in 23 games and scoring one goal) but Terry was not getting any younger, and in June 1979, after a rather indifferent last season with the Potters (just nine outings, five as a substitute, mainly because of knee problems) he chose to try a new venture by joining Bulova FC in Hong Kong.

During his time with Stoke, Terry gained 26 full caps for the Republic of Ireland, the first against Czechoslovakia, and was in fact the first Stoke City player to represent the Republic since the Emerald Isle split into two footballing nations. He did reasonably well in Hong Kong (so he said) before returning to England to sign for Crewe Alexandra on a free transfer in January 1980. Terry retired in June 1981 at the age of 34 having added a further 37 League appearances to his overall tally.

Terry began concentrating wholly on his own business in the Potteries, but still turned out in several local charity matches for the Stoke City over-35s side. He later returned to the club he served so well for 12 years as a matchday host and is now a commercial executive at the Britannia Stadium, contributing regularly to the matchday programme.

Ian Cranson

Born: Easington, County Durham, 2 July 1964

Stoke City record:
Appearances: League 220+3, FA Cup 14, League Cup 16+1, others 27
Goals: League 9, FA Cup 1, League Cup 1, others 1
Debut: League, 19 August 1989 v West Ham United (h) drew 1–1

Also played for: Ipswich Town, Sheffield Wednesday, England (5 Under-21 caps)

Defender Ian Cranson made 165 first-class appearances for Ipswich Town, whom he joined initially as an apprentice in July 1980, turning professional two years later, and going on to gain England Under-21 recognition. He joined Sheffield Wednesday at the age of 23 but suffered with injuries during his 16 months at Hillsborough (35 outings) before moving to Stoke City for a then record fee of £450,000 in March 1988. He regained full fitness with the Potters and went on to play in 281 first-class games over the next eight and a half years, gaining an Autoglass Trophy-winner's medal in 1992 and a Second Division Championship-winners' medal a year later. A solid, reliable performer, he was rewarded with a testimonial by Stoke after amassing a career record of 481 club appearances and scoring 15 goals.

Ian made his League debut for Ipswich in December 1983 against Aston Villa at a time when Russell Osman and Terry Butcher were the regular central-defenders at Portman Road. At Hillsborough his back four partners included Nigel Pearson and Lawrie Madden, but he was never happy with the Owls, hence his move to the Victoria Ground.

Owing to the excellent form of centre-backs George Berry and Steve Bould, and then John Higgins and Berry, Ian had to wait until the opening day of the 1989–90 season for his first senior game for the Potters, lining up alongside Chris Kamara against West Ham United at home. He did well in the 1–1 draw and

played in 19 matches before suffering knee ligament damage against Bournemouth at Dean Court in mid-November.

Ian missed the rest of the season and most of 1990–91 before damaging his other knee against Mansfield Town in March. At the end of that season Ian was offered reduced terms in his contract with the club, which technically entitled him to a free transfer, but despite the interest shown by Scottish Premiership clubs Dunfermline Athletic and Hearts, he chose to remain at the Victoria Ground.

As resilient as ever, he persevered via the treatment room, gaining tremendous respect and admiration as he slowly but surely clawed his way back to full fitness.

At the start of the 1991–92 campaign he duly returned to first-team action under manager Lou Macari, as confident and resourceful as ever. After just one game at left-back, he was handed the unfamiliar number-seven shirt. With Noel Blake, Vince Overson and Lee Sandford all capable of playing in the heart of the defence, Ian battled on, making 57 League and Cup appearances in total and helping the Potters storm through to Wembley in the Final of the Autoglass Trophy. There they met and beat Stockport County 1–0 in front of 48,339 spectators, the highlight of Ian's career at that point.

The following season, playing alongside Overson, he missed only one League game as the Potters clinched promotion to the 'new' First Division as champions.

In 1993–94 he was a near ever present, missing only two League matches, while the following season he was absent on nine occasions, mainly through niggling pains and twinges in his dodgy knees which would continue to plague him for the remainder of his career, severely restricting his pace and mobility. Yet he never moaned, he simply got on with the job of defending and did it with total commitment and endeavour.

Ian continued to play for the Potters on a regular basis through to the end of the 1995–96 season. He managed just a handful of games the following term before finally announcing his retirement on medical advice in November 1996. He later returned to the club as a coach and now looks after the youth team, a true and dedicated Potter to this day. Ian was a truly grand club man, a player who never gave in, whether he was playing out on the pitch or under the guidance of the physiotherapist in the treatment room.

Garth Crooks

Born: 10 March 1958, Stoke-on-Trent

Stoke City record:
Appearances: League 141+6, FA Cup 3+2, League Cup 10+2
Goals: League 48, FA Cup 1, League Cup 4
Debut: League, 10 April 1976 v Coventry City (h) lost 1–0

Also played for: Tottenham Hotspur, Manchester United, West Bromwich Albion,
                    Charlton Athletic, England (4 Under-21 caps)

Garth Crooks was a snappy little striker with a good turn of pace, and a scorer of some stunning goals. He joined his home-town club, Stoke City, as a 16-year-old in 1974, signed by manager Tony Waddington who, it is said, used to watch Garth kicking a ball against a wall outside the Victoria Ground!

After some impressive displays in the youth and reserve teams, Garth turned professional in March 1976 at a time when black footballers were rare. His initiation into the hard, sometimes cruel world of professional sports was made more of a trial by the virulent, unceasing abuse that came echoing down from the terraces.

Garth commented afterwards 'If you couldn't cope, you fell foul of the industry. No black player has been spared it – one has to deal with it and get on with it because sport offers an opportunity, one of the few areas where you can get on, doing what you do best, where talent is allowed to come through.'

He made his senior debut for the Potters against Coventry a month after becoming a professional – the first of 164 appearances he made for Stoke over a period of nine years up to March 1976, when he was transferred to Tottenham Hotspur for £600,000. He also scored 53 goals, including a hat-trick against his future club, West Bromwich Albion, in December 1979.

His best season in terms of goals scored came in 1977–78, when he struck 19 in 45 games. He netted 13 the following season and 15 in his last, helping Stoke regain their top-flight status by finishing third behind Crystal Palace and Brighton in Division Two.

Garth was capped four times by England at Under-21 level in 1979–80, lining up against Bulgaria, Scotland twice and Germany, and to celebrate his first cap he scored a hat-trick in a 5–0 win over the Bulgarians at Leicester.

He teamed up with Steve Archibald in the Spurs attack and went on to score 77 goals in 182 appearances, finding the net in eight consecutive games in 1984 to equal the club record. He won two FA Cup-winners' medals with Spurs in 1981, when he scored the equaliser prior to Ricky Villa's memorable winner against Manchester City, and in 1982 against QPR. He also collected a League Cup runners'-up medal against Liverpool in 1982 and a UEFA Cup medal in the same year.

After a short loan spell with Manchester United (November 1983–January 1984) he spent almost two years with West Bromwich Albion (July 1985–March 1987) and three more at Charlton Athletic before injury ended his career in May 1990. In 14 years as a professional, Garth scored 171 goals in 473 club appearances.

Garth has always been an activist. In 1985 he founded SCAR, the Sickle Cell Anaemia Relief Organisation, to promote awareness of the illness and to raise funds for medical research and to support sufferers. In fact, since the early 1980s he has been involved in various forms of community work, including liaising with the Metropolitan Police, serving on the Notting Hill Carnival committee and working with various London Boys' clubs to promote community values through football. In the latter sense, he was perfectly in tune with a major PFA initiative of the 1980s – the Football in the Community programme.

Currently chairman of the Football Foundation's Grass Roots Advisory Group, Garth was awarded the OBE for his services to the Institute of Professional Sport in June 1999.

He has served on the BBC's World Cup TV panel and throughout the 1980s was regularly seen and heard in a variety of guises on both TV and radio programmes, co-hosting a *Top of the Pops* show in 1982, presenting BBC2's late night *Despatch Box*, while his discussion-cum-record show on Greater London Radio won him a Sony Award.

In the early 1990s he was producing and presenting football programmes on Channel 4 and is now an integral part of the BBC *Match of the Day* team. He was also elected the first black chairman of the PFA in 1988 – the 100th anniversary of the Football League.

Harry Davies

Born:	29 January 1904, Gainsborough, Lincolnshire
Died:	23 April 1975, Blurton, Stoke-on-Trent

Stoke City record:

Appearances:	League 388, FA Cup 22
Goals:	League 92, FA Cup 9
Debut:	League, 23 September 1922 v West Bromwich Albion (h) lost 2–0

Also played for: Bamfords Athletic, Huddersfield Town, Port Vale

The son of the former Hull City, Shrewsbury Town, Doncaster Rovers, Gainsborough Trinity and Wolverhampton Wanderers full-back of the same name, Harry Augustus Davies was educated in Gainsborough and played non-League football for the Uttoxeter-based club Bamfords Athletic before joining Stoke as a full-time professional in June 1922. He spent seven years at the Victoria Ground before moving to Huddersfield Town in May 1929, later returning to Stoke for a second spell in February 1932 and then ending his career with neighbours Port Vale with whom he stayed from February 1938 to April 1939.

An aggressive, all-action and confident forward, able to lead the attack or occupy an inside berth, Harry averaged a goal every four games for the Potters. He possessed loads of ability and always looked the part on the field, regularly taking the ball into a precarious position before suddenly opening up the play with a superbly measured cross-field pass or a swift body movement. He was without doubt a class act, and he gave supporters plenty to cheer about during his two spells at the club, finding the net at least once in each of his 13 seasons in the first XI at the Victoria Ground.

He struck five times in 24 games in his initial campaign (1922–23, when sadly the Potters were relegated) and followed up with nine goals in 32 outings in 1923–24. Thereafter he netted regularly, including 13 in 32 starts in 1925–26 when the team dropped out of the Second Division for the first time in the club's history; 17 in 42 appearances when the Third Division North title was won at the first attempt in 1926–27; and five in 33 games when the Second Division Championship was won in 1932–33.

When helping the Potters regain their Second Division status in 1927, Harry played brilliantly alongside Charlie Wilson and Johnny Eyres. Between them they netted over 50 League goals, Wilson top-scoring with 25, half of which were made by Harry Davies.

Harry was in great form again in 1932–33 when the Potters lifted the Second Division title, but by this time he was playing more as a schemer than a goal-getter and laid on chances galore for Joe Mawson, Tommy Sale and Joe Johnson.

Twice a Staffordshire County representative in matches against the Football League in 1926 and 1927, Harry came close to gaining a full England cap in 1929 but missed out to West Bromwich Albion's Joe Carter. He was named a reserve for an international match at Sheffield and during the summer of that year toured South Africa with the FA party, playing in two Test Matches against the host country, having left the Victoria Ground to join Huddersfield Town in May.

The manager who signed him was Herbert Chapman, who wanted a quality player to partner Clem Stephenson on the right wing. Harry fitted the bill a treat and quickly settled in at Leeds Road, appearing in that season's FA Cup Final against Arsenal, which Huddersfield lost 2–0.

After scoring 17 goals in 55 games for the Yorkshire club, Harry returned to Stoke in February 1932. He played on for another six years, taking his appearance tally for the club to 410 and his goal count to 101, reaching the century mark with a cracker in a 3–1 win over Birmingham in February 1936.

After spending a season in Stoke's second XI (Jimmy Westland replaced him in the first team), Harry moved to Port Vale in a deal that saw Tommy Ward switch to the Victoria Ground. He made 45 appearances for the Valiants before retiring in April 1939 at the age of 35.

Besides being a wonderful footballer, one of the best to serve Stoke City, Harry Davies was also a fine snooker and billiards player and recorded seven century breaks, his best effort being 135.

Lee Dixon

Born:	17 March 1964, Manchester

Stoke City record:

Appearances:	League 71, FA Cup 7, League Cup 6, others 4
Goals:	League 5
Debut:	League, 23 August 1986 v Birmingham City (h) lost 2–0
Also played for:	Burnley, Chester City, Bury, Arsenal, England (4 B and 22 full caps)

Lee Dixon worked his way to the top of the football ladder slowly but effectively, eventually developing into a world-class player. He started out with Burnley, where he served his apprenticeship, before turning professional in July 1982. He was transferred to Chester City in February 1984 and played for Bury from July 1985 before joining Stoke City for £40,000 in the summer of 1986.

He took over the then troublesome right-back position from Aaron Callaghan and, after a rather disappointing debut game against Birmingham City, he went on to become an ever present in his first season with the Potters, who finished eighth in the Second Division.

The following season Lee had played in 29 League and nine Cup ties before he was, perhaps surprisingly, sold to Arsenal in January 1988, manager George Graham paying £400,000 for his signature – 10 times the amount Stoke boss Mick Mills had paid for him two years earlier. He was signed after Viv Anderson left the Gunners for Manchester United.

Lee had amassed 88 senior appearances for the Potters and scored three goals, all in home League games in 1986–87 against Leeds United (won 7–2), Crystal Palace (won 3–1) and Sunderland (won 3–0).

However, Lee had to wait some seven months before gaining a regular place in the Arsenal line up after manager Graham decided to switch Nigel Winterburn to the right to partner Kenny Sansom. Lee made only six appearances in his first season before bedding himself down alongside Winterburn after Sansom's departure, and the two became regarded as the best pair of full-backs at club level anywhere in the world.

Captain and long-serving centre-back David O'Leary operated in the middle of the defence and was soon joined by another former Stoke player, Steve Bould, as Arsenal became serious challengers for the First Division title in 1989.

Lee was a marauding right-back, ever willing to support his winger, and his attacking skills were still noted even though his main job (and the main priority of the side as a whole) was to defend. He helped the Gunners win the League title on the last day of the 1988–89 season at Anfield, helping set up a dramatic late winner for Michael Thomas.

This was the first of many honours Lee would win as a Gunner. In his 14½ years at Highbury he played in 614 competitive matches, over 450 at League level. He won a second League Championship medal in 1991, collected two Premiership medals (1998 and 2002), was successful in three FA Cup Finals (1993, 1998 and 2002), won the European Cup-Winners' Cup (1994) and twice helped Arsenal win the FA Charity Shield (1998 and 1999). He missed the 1993 League Cup Final after being sent off in the semi-final against Spurs (at Wembley). He also earned four B and 22 full caps for England, and when he retired at the age of 38 he had amassed 860 club and international appearances – a magnificent record.

His full England debut came in April 1990 in a World Cup warm-up game against Czechoslovakia, and his last international followed some nine years later against France. He also scored a goal at Wembley in his sixth international in an important Euro '92 qualifier against the Republic of Ireland. The game ended 1–1. Lee retired after Arsenal had completed the League and Cup double in 2002. He was 38 years of age at the time.

Divorced and in retirement, Lee has concentrated on several business interests, including the Riverside Brasserie in Bray, Berkshire, originally with his friend Heston Blumenthal. He enjoys a daily round of golf, hoping to reduce his handicap at the Woburn club. He is also a pundit for the BBC, appearing on flagship football shows *Match of the Day*, *Score* and *Football Focus*.

Bob Dixon

Born:	30 August 1904, Easington near Whitehaven
Died:	c.1980, Stoke-on-Trent

Stoke City record:

Appearances:	League 189, FA Cup 11
Debut:	League, 22 January 1923 v Blackburn Rovers (a) won 5–1

Also played for: West Stanley, West Ham United

Bob Dixon was a courageous goalkeeper who performed splendidly in non-League football for West Stanley before joining Stoke in January 1923. At the time the Potters were struggling on the field and were heading feet first into the Second Division. They were also leaking goals like nobody's business and in fact the club had used no fewer than seven 'keepers since the resumption of League football in 1919.

The club's directors had been informed of 18-year-old Bob by their eagle-eyed scout in County Durham, who some years earlier had spotted Dick Herron plying his trade with West Stanley. After a couple of spying missions in the North East, Bob was recruited by the Potters for a small fee. Signed initially as cover for Les Scott, he immediately made his League debut in a resounding 5–1 win away to Blackburn Rovers in front of 10,000 spectators. This was Stoke's first away victory since March 1922 and Bob proceeded to gain rave reports for his efforts in the second XI. He eventually established himself in the Potters' first XI a third of the way into the 1923–24 season despite fierce competition from the experienced Scottish international Kenny Campbell, who had arrived at the Victoria Ground two months after Bob.

Bob was to stay at the Victoria Ground for a little over six years and in that time he amassed exactly 200 appearances at competitive level, and was rated as one of the best 'keepers outside the First Division in the mid to late 1920s. He was outstanding during the last half of 1923–24, helping the Potters claim sixth spot in the Second Division. That term he made 31 appearances and conceded only 26 goals, a fifth of them coming in a comprehensive 5–1 defeat at Crystal Palace, Stoke's worst reverse of the campaign.

In 1924–25 he made 34 first-team appearances as the Potters battled in vain to get out of the Second Division. The following season, despite Bob producing some excellent performances, the Potters were relegated to the Third Division North for the first time in the club's history.

Things could only get better – and they did. Bob missed only one game, the penultimate one of the season against Lincoln City, as the Potters clinched promotion and with it the Third Division North Championship at the first attempt.

In his other 41 games Bob generally played very well, especially in the away wins at Accrington, Ashington, Crewe, Durham (the club he supported as a lad), Walsall and Wigan Borough. He also made some brilliant home performances against Barrow, Lincoln City and Southport, and he saved three penalties (two of them crucial) during the course of the campaign. In all, he kept 18 clean sheets in 1926–27.

Bob was again absent just once in season 1927–28, missing the 2–1 win at Grimsby in early March but comfortably retaining his place in the side. However, after seven outings at the start of 1928–29 Bob was replaced between the posts by Dick Williams, who had been in reserve during the previous two campaigns. He remained at the Victoria Ground until March 1929.

Bob moved to West Ham, acting as reserve to Ted Hufton, and got into their first team towards the end of the following season, making 12 appearances, and after that he shared the goalkeeping duties with Hufton until George Watson and Pat McMahon both arrived on the scene. Having made 68 appearances for the London club, Bob left Upton Park in May 1933 to return to his roots in Durham, where he became a labourer on a coalfield. Throughout his career for Stoke, Bob kept 63 clean sheets in 200 appearances – a 32 per cent record.

Peter Dobing

Born:　　　1 December 1938, Manchester

Stoke City record:
Appearances:　League 303+4, FA Cup 22, League Cup 39+1, others 3
Goals:　　　League 82, FA Cup 3, League Cup 9
Debut:　　　League, 24 August 1963 v Tottenham Hotspur (h) won 2–1

Also played for:　Crewe Rangers, Blackburn Rovers, Manchester City, Parkway FC, Cleveland Stokers (NASL)

Peter Dobing came from a sporting family, as his father played rugby league for Salford and other relations enjoyed football and cricket. He started his soccer career with Blackburn Rovers, signing as an amateur in 1953 and turning professional in December 1955. He made his League debut as a 17-year-old alongside England's Bryan Douglas in September 1956 and in season 1957–58 scored 25 competitive goals, including four in one match against Bristol City, helping Rovers gain promotion to the First Division as runners-up. The following season he netted 26 times, the highest return of his career, and in 1959–60 played a large part in Blackburn's run to the FA Cup Final. He scored five goals during that Cup run, but failed to hit the target at Wembley as Rovers were soundly beaten 3–0 by Wolverhampton Wanderers.

In July 1961, after scoring 104 goals in 205 outings for the Ewood Park club, Peter moved to Manchester City for a fee of £38,000, signed as a straight replacement for Denis Law, who had departed for the Italian club Torino. He made his City debut on the opening day of the 1961–62 season, starring in a 3–1 win over Leicester City. He started all but one of City's matches that season, finishing up as the club's top scorer with 22 goals. The following season he was less successful and netted only 10 times in 50 appearances in a year that ended in bitter disappointment as City were relegated to the Second Division.

As a result Peter was sold to newly promoted Stoke City in August 1963, signed by manager Tony Waddington for the sum of £37,500. He had an excellent first season with the Potters, lining up alongside Stanley Matthews, Dennis Viollet, John Ritchie and Jimmy McIlroy and helping them reach the Final of the League Cup, but unfortunately he had to settle for a runners'-up prize as City were beaten 4–3 on aggregate by Leicester.

Peter spent more than a decade at the Victoria Ground and gave the club yeoman service. Although he probably had a love-hate relationship with the club, he was nevertheless greatly admired by the fans, who saw him produce some terrific performances as an attacking forward, sometimes as a scheming inside-right and occasionally as a makeshift winger. Perhaps one of his finest displays in a Stoke shirt was when he scored a stunning hat-trick in a 3–2 home League win over Leeds United in April 1968. The fans who were present that day will never forget how he ran England's centre-half Jack Charlton and his co-defenders ragged.

He captained the team that beat Chelsea 2–1 to win the League Cup at Wembley in 1972 (and so bring Stoke their first major trophy). Peter was well known for his short temper, especially on the pitch, which got him in trouble with officialdom more than once – one incident resulted in him receiving a nine-week suspension, an English record at that time.

Close to winning a full England cap on several occasions, Peter was selected to star in seven Under-23 internationals for his country as a Blackburn player between 1959 and 1961. He also represented the Football League on two occasions in 1959–60.

His playing career effectively ended after he suffered a broken leg in 1973. Although he regained his fitness and returned to Stoke's first team, he was never the same player again and quit the professional arena at the age of 35. He later assisted Parkway (in a few games) and had a brief spell with NASL club Cleveland Stokers before hanging up his boots for good.

Besides being a very fine footballer, Peter was also an extremely capable cricketer. He scored plenty of runs and once took the field in a County game as 12th man for Lancashire against Yorkshire in the annual Roses match. He later worked in the Staffordshire pottery industry at Longton.

Alan Dodd

Born: 20 September 1953, Stoke-on-Trent

Stoke City record:
Appearances: League 365+7, FA Cup 15, League Cup 25, others 4
Goals: League 3, League Cup 1
Debut: League, 4 November 1972 v Sheffield United (a) drew 0–0

Also played for: Wolverhampton Wanderers, Elfsborg (2 spells), GAIS Gothenberg, Port Vale, Cork City, Landskrona Bols, Rocester (2 spells as player and player-coach), Goldenhill Wanderers, Ball Haye Green WMC, England (6 Under-23 caps)

Alan Dodd joined forces with Denis Smith at the heart of the Stoke City defence during the 1974–75 campaign and the pair starred together for five seasons before the latter's career began to wind down. Alan remained a vital member of the team and, with Mick Doyle alongside him, continued to perform well until his transfer to Wolverhampton Wanderers in November 1982.

Initially a midfielder, Alan signed for the Potters as an apprentice in April 1968 and turned professional in October 1969. After some spirited performances in the reserves, in a variety of positions including right-back, centre-half and central midfield, he made his League debut in a goalless draw away to Sheffield United while still a teenager (autumn 1972).

During 1973–74 Alan made 38 senior appearances, wearing seven different shirt numbers, and the following season he moved into the heart of the Stoke defence on a regular basis, taking over from the formidable Alan Bloor.

Always highly regarded by manager Tony Waddington, Alan was strong and reliable both in the air and on the ground, although it must be said, and he agreed to a certain extent, that he tended to lose concentration at times, and perhaps this was the reason he did not win more honours for his country than the seven Under-23 caps gained between 1974 and 1976. He lined up against Czechoslovakia (twice), Portugal (twice), Hungary, Scotland and Wales. Jimmy Greenhoff, Alan Hudson, Ian Moores and future 'Stokie' John Gidman all played with him in games against the Czechs and Magyars, while another player with a Stoke connection, Dennis Tueart, also starred against Scotland.

An ever present in 1976–77 and 1977–78, Alan had a tremendous run of 113 consecutive first-team outings (including one as a substitute) for the Potters between 10 January 1976 and 29 April 1978. In this time he scored his first goal for the club to earn a point from a 1–1 draw with Leeds United at Elland Road in the relegation campaign of 1976–77 in which the Potters, to be truthful, were appalling, winning only 10 of the 42 First Division games and scoring just 21 goals.

Alan was certainly one of the mainstays of the side from September 1973 until May 1982. In that time the Potters completed a total of 426 competitive matches and Alan played in 395 of them. He was in excellent form when promotion was gained in 1978–79 and was voted the club's Player of the Year the following season. It must be said, however, that Alan was lucky not to suffer too many injuries, missing most of his games through suspension and illness.

After making exactly 400 appearances for the Potters and receiving a well-deserved testimonial match (against Port Vale), Alan moved to Molineux for £40,000 and stayed until January 1985, making 99 appearances for Wolves and helping them regain their First Division status.

When he returned to Stoke, Bill Asprey was the manager and Alan added just 16 more first-class appearances to his tally before opting to join Swedish club Elfsborg in July 1985. He later had a second spell with that same club and in December 1986 assisted Port Vale in two games as a loan player before eventually drifting down the football ladder and slipping into non-League circles.

Alan's senior career with his three English, one Irish and three Swedish clubs realised 563 appearances, 462 of them in the Football League. He was associated with Stoke City football club for a total of 14 years.

Mike Doyle

Born: 25 November 1946, Manchester

Stoke City record:
Appearances: League 115, FA Cup 5, League Cup 8
Goals: League 5, League Cup 1
Debut: League, 19 August 1978 v Cambridge United (a) won 1–0

Also played for: Manchester City, Bolton Wanderers, Rochdale, England (8
                   Under-23 and 5 full caps)

Mike Doyle started kicking a ball around when he was three years old and continued to do so for the next 35 years, appearing for four League clubs as well as his country and the Football League while accumulating a splendid personal record of 771 senior appearances and 51 goals. He joined the groundstaff at Maine Road on leaving school in the summer of 1962 and turned professional with Manchester City in May 1964.

In his early days with his home-town club, Mike donned the number-nine shirt when playing in the second XI, but it would be as a midfielder and defender that he eventually made his mark. He made his Football League debut at left-half against Cardiff City in March 1965 (replacing Alan Oakes) and went on to serve City for a total of 16 years before his transfer to Stoke City for what was to prove a bargain fee of £50,000 in June 1978.

Regarded as one of Manchester City's finest-ever players, Mike was certainly at his best under Manchester City's managership partnership of Malcolm Allison and Joe Mercer and then later when Tony Book was at the helm.

A determined performer, hard in the tackle, his influence helped the Blues win the Second Division Championship in 1965–66 (when he scored seven goals in 20 outings), the First Division in 1967–68, the FA Charity Shield soon afterwards, the FA Cup in 1969, the League Cup in 1970 (when he netted the equaliser in the 2–1 extra-time victory over West Bromwich Albion), the European Cup-Winners' Cup against Gornik Zabrze in Vienna and the 1976 League Cup Final against Newcastle United, when his teammates included Dennis Tueart, Asa Hartford and Dave Watson, all of whom would later be associated with the Potters. Mike was also in City's 1974 losing League Cup Final side against Wolves.

In between times he gained five full England caps, against Wales, Scotland, Brazil and Italy in 1976 and Holland in 1977. He also played in eight Under-23 internationals (in 1968 and 1969) and twice represented the Football League against the Scottish League, in 1972 and 1976. He also appeared for an England XI against Team America in 1976.

In the summer of 1978, after struggling with injuries and losing his place in the City team to Tommy Booth, Mike joined Stoke City, signed by Alan Durban. Mike fitted straight into the team alongside Denis Smith at the heart of the defence and helped the Potters win the Second Division title in his first season, missing only one game. The following season he missed several matches through illness and suspension but his presence on the field certainly boosted and encouraged the younger players as the Potters consolidated themselves in the top flight.

In 1980–81 he was back to his best, this time forming a fine defensive partnership with Alan Dodd. He also netted four goals, including one against his former club Manchester City in mid-March as the Potters won 2–1. Earlier, he struck in successive draws with Coventry City and Crystal Palace and found the net again to earn a point away to Birmingham City.

Mike certainly gave the Potters excellent service for three and a half years before returning to Lancashire to join Bolton Wanderers for £10,000 in January 1982 – this after Smith had returned from injury and Dave Watson was signed from Southampton.

In his first two games for the Trotters, Mike conceded an own-goal against Oldham Athletic and was sent off at Newcastle United. He ended his playing career with Rochdale, whom he served from August 1983–May 1984. In later years Mike became a sales manager for the sports company Slazenger and also covered local football matches on Piccadilly Radio. He now lives in Ashton-under-Lyne.

George Eastham, OBE

Born: 23 September 1936, Blackpool

Stoke City record:
Appearances: League 184+10, FA Cup 23, League Cup 17+2, others 2+1
Goals: League 4, League Cup 1
Debut: League, 20 August 1966 v Nottingham Forest (a) won 2–1

Also played for: Bispham Church, Highfield Youth Club, Blackpool (trial), Bolton
                Wanderers (trial), Ards, Newcastle United, Arsenal, Cleveland
                Stokers (NASL), Cape Town Spurs, Hellenic FC (player-manager),
                England (6 Under-23 and 19 full caps)
Also managed: Stoke City

George Eastham represented Blackpool Schools, assisted two local youth teams and had unsuccessful trials with both Blackpool and Bolton Wanderers before joining the Northern Ireland club Ards as an amateur in April 1954, turning professional in September 1955.

He developed quickly and played alongside his father, also named George, in Ireland. After being watched by a number of big-name clubs, George junior was eventually approached by Newcastle United scout Bill McCracken and joined for a fee of £9,000 in May 1956 aged 19, signed by manager Stan Seymour.

He spent four and a half years at St James' Park, flourishing alongside cultured Welsh international Ivor Allchurch in midfield. Performing equally well on the left or right, George became the new star on Tyneside but then became involved in an unsavoury affair with the North East club, first regarding money and a house and secondly by standing up for his belief that he should be able to ply his trade as a footballer where he liked. Backed by the Player's Union, George took football's antiquated authorities and the rule book, as well as Newcastle United Football Club, to the High Court and won an historic battle to free, as the media then called footballers, the 'soccer slaves'.

By the time the long drawn out legal process was resolved (in 1963) George had already been granted permission to leave Newcastle, joining Arsenal in October 1960 for a fee of £47,500 and becoming the second most expensive footballer in Britain. He scored 34 goals in 129 games for the Geordies.

He spent six years at Highbury and netted 41 times in 223 appearances, as well as being called up to the England squads for the 1962 and 1966 World Cup Finals. More often than not he was classed as a reserve for the national team, winning only 19 full caps, the first against Brazil in 1963, the last against Denmark in 1966, plus six Under-23 caps. He also played in five unofficial internationals and represented the Football League.

George switched his allegiance from Arsenal to Stoke City in a £30,000 deal in August 1966. He remained a 'Potter' until February 1971, when he flew out to South Africa to join Cape Town Spurs on loan as player-coach. He was then appointed player-manager of another South African side, Hellenic FC, only to return to his former club, Stoke City, as a player in October 1971. He took over as assistant manager two months later before announcing his retirement as a player in March 1977. He continued as manager at that point, retaining office until January 1978, when he emigrated to South Africa and started his own sportswear business in Johannesburg called 'Hat Trick'. He was also appointed vice-president of the Arsenal supporters' club.

As a Stoke player, George partnered Harry Burrows on the left wing and missed only one League game in his first season and three in his second before injuries interrupted his performances in 1968–69. He came back strongly the following season when he teamed up with Terry Conroy, Peter Dobing and Jimmy Greenhoff in midfield, but after that his form waned before he left for a brief sojourn in Cape Town.

After his return, he went on to amass a total of 239 senior appearances for the Potters, striking five goals including the crucial winner in the 1972 League Cup Final against Chelsea at the age of 35 years and 161 days.

Unfortunately, he did not do too well as a manager at the Victoria Ground but he certainly made an impact in South Africa with his coaching and general football brain. He was awarded the OBE for services to football in 1975. George, who wanted to leave a financial legacy to his children, sold his personal collection of football memorabilia in June 2008.

George's father played for Bolton Wanderers (amateur), Brentford, Blackpool, Lincoln City, Rochdale, Swansea, Hyde United, Ards and England (one cap) and also served as a scout for Stoke City. His uncle, Henry, played for Accrington Stanley, Blackpool, Liverpool and Tranmere Rovers.

Tony Ford, MBE

Born: 14 May 1959, Grimsby

Stoke City record:
Appearances: League 112, FA Cup 9, League Cup 8, others 6
Goals: League 13, others 1
Debut: League, 23 August 1986 v Birmingham City (h) lost 2–0

Also played for: Sunderland, Grimsby Town, Bradford City, West Bromwich
                     Albion, Scunthorpe United, Mansfield Town, Rochdale, Barrow,
                     England B (2 caps)

Throughout most of his career, Tony Ford played as a right-sided midfielder, but in the later years he was converted to a very resourceful and composed right-back.

Over a period of 26 years, from the day of his debut as a second-half substitute in the League game for Grimsby Town against Walsall in October 1975 until his retirement as a full-time professional in November 2001, Tony played in no less than 931 League matches, which remains the all-time record for appearances in the competition by an outfield player (only goalkeeper Peter Shilton, with 1,005 matches, has played more). His 118 Cup games, 31 other fixtures and two England B internationals add up to a grand total of 1,082 senior appearances. He also weighed in with 120 goals.

Tony is, in fact, the only outfield player in English football to have passed the milestone of 1,000 games in competitive matches, and the only Football League ground he never played on (when registered as a full-time professional) was White Hart Lane.

Tony began his career at his home-town club Grimsby Town, where he made his first-team debut as a 16-year-old. He spent 11 years at Blundell Park, where he made his name as one of the most talented players outside the top division. In July 1986, after a loan spell with Sunderland, he signed for Stoke City for £35,000.

He spent two and a half years with the Potters, missing only one League game in his first season, being an ever present in his second and playing in 27 out of 30 games in 1988–89. He was transferred to West Bromwich Albion in March 1989 for £135,000 and, after spending a further two and a half years at The Hawthorns, he rejoined Grimsby for £50,000 in November 1991. His second spell with the Mariners lasted three seasons, and when he left at the end of the 1993–94 season he had appeared in 423 League games for the Cleethorpes club, which at the time placed him second in the Mariners' career appearance list behind Keith Jobling (he has since been passed in that list by John McDermott and Paul Groves).

In August 1994, following a loan spell with Bradford City, Tony joined Grimsby's arch-rivals Scunthorpe United, where he played two seasons. When he was released at the end of the 1995–96 campaign, it seemed like his career at League level had come to an end. However, after a short spell with non-League side Barrow he was asked by Steve Parkin, a former teammate at Stoke and West Bromwich Albion who had recently been appointed manager at Mansfield Town, to become his assistant at Field Mill. This allowed Tony to continue his playing career and, in early 1999, he played in his 825th League game, thus breaking Terry Paine's then existing record for career appearances by an outfield player.

In the summer of 1999, Parkin resigned as Mansfield manager to take a similar job at Rochdale. Once again, he appointed Tony as his assistant and, despite being well past 40, Tony continued to play on a regular basis. He finally retired from playing in November 2001 when he and Parkin took up the same positions at Barnsley, understandably feeling himself unequal to Division One football.

Unfortunately, he was sacked along with Parkin 11 months after taking office but in August 2003 he returned to his old role at Rochdale under new manager Alan Buckley. He kept his job when Buckley made way for Parkin on 31 December 2003 but the pair were dismissed three years later.

Tony was awarded the MBE for services to football in 2000.

Peter Fox

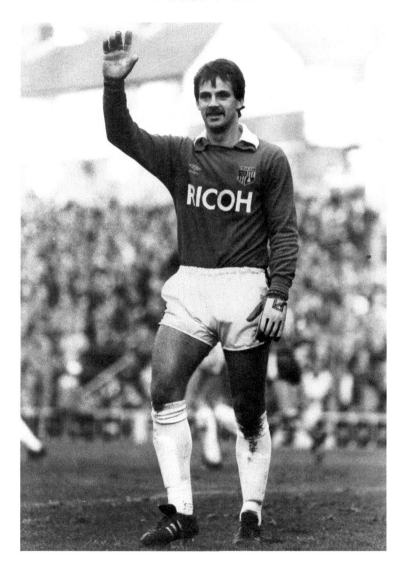

Born:	5 July 1957, Scunthorpe

Stoke City record:

Appearances:	League 409, FA Cup 22, League Cup 32, others 14
Debut:	League, 16 December 1978 v Leyton Orient (h) won 3–0

Also played for: Sheffield Wednesday, West Ham United, Barnsley, Team Hawaii (NASL), Linfield, Exeter City (player-manager)

Goalkeeper Peter Fox was a very consistent and, indeed, reliable performer throughout his career. Never the flashy type, he did the simple things easily while also dealing with the harder tasks efficiently and competently. He was only 15 years and eight months old when he made his Football League debut for Sheffield Wednesday against Leyton Orient in a Second Division game in 1973 – the youngest player ever to appear in a senior game for the Yorkshire club, whom he joined initially as an apprentice in July 1972, turning professional in June 1975.

He had his best run in Wednesday's first XI during the second half of the 1975–76 season (playing in 28 first-class matches), but after loan spells with West Ham United and Barnsley and a spell in the NASL with Team Hawaii he joined Stoke City in March 1978, when Chris Turner established himself between the posts at Hillsborough.

Signed for just £15,000 by manager Alan Durban, Peter was reserve to Roger Jones and had to wait until mid-December 1978 before making his debut for the Potters in a 3–0 home League win over Wrexham. He eventually took over the number-one spot (from Jones) halfway through the 1979–80 season and remained first choice between the posts until November 1984, when a niggling back injury was causing him some concern. He fought on, regained full fitness and returned to pole position in 1985–86, retaining it for two seasons before giving way to Scott Barrett after suffering more problems with his back

A fighter to the last, Peter became a first-team regular again in 1988–89, retaining his position until 1991, when he was replaced by Jason Kearton. At this juncture, Ronnie Sinclair was also registered with the club and soon afterwards Sheffield Wednesday's goalkeeper, Kevin Pressman, arrived at the Victoria Ground on loan as Peter's back problem to continued to annoy him.

An ever present in seasons 1980–81 and 1983–84, Peter was very popular with the Stoke City supporters and earned himself a testimonial for his loyal and dedicated service. The recipient of a full FA coaching badge, Peter holds the record for the most senior appearances ever made by a goalkeeper for the club – 477 – and he also kept 139 clean sheets for the Potters. He is currently sixth in the club's all-time list for appearances, with only Eric Skeels, John McCue, Bob McGrory, Denis Smith and Alan Bloor ahead of him.

Peter helped Stoke win the Autoglass Trophy against Stockport County at Wembley in May 1992 and clinch the Second Division Championship the following year, although he only appeared in 10 League matches – Sinclair was regarded as first choice most of the time while Bruce Grobbelaar also had a few outings.

Peter remained at the Victoria Ground until July 1993, when he left on a free transfer to become player-coach under his former Stoke City manager Alan Ball at Exeter City. He took over as player-manager of the Grecians in June 1995 and retired as a player at the end of that season, but he remained in charge at St James Park until May 2000. Unfortunately, Peter did not have the happiest of times in charge of Exeter, who twice escaped relegation from Division Three by the skin of their Devon teeth! He was replaced in the proverbial hot seat by former Potters defender Noel Blake, who had played in front of Peter during the early 1990s.

Peter later served as a goalkeeping coach and part-time scout for Rochdale before taking over as goalkeeping coach at Blackpool, who went to the new Wembley in May 2007 and beat Yeovil Town in the League One Play-off Final. Peter's son, David, came on as a second-half midfield substitute.

Neil Franklin

Born: 24 January 1922, Stoke-on-Trent
Died: 17 February 1996, Stoke-on-Trent

Stoke City record:
Appearances: League 142, FA Cup 20, wartime 186
Goals: Wartime 3
Debut: Wartime, 18 May 1940 v Everton (a) lost 1–0
                FA Cup, 5 January 1946 v Burnley (h) won 3–1

Also played for: Stoke Old Boys, (wartime guest for Gainsborough Trinity),
                  Independienté Sante Fé (Colombia), Hull City, Crewe Alexandra,
                  Stockport County, Macclesfield Town, Wellington Town, GKN
                  Sankey's (player-manager), England (1 B, 10 wartime and 27 full caps)
Managed: Colchester United

Cornelius 'Neil' Franklin played for his school team, in local junior football and for Stoke Old Boys before joining the groundstaff at the Victoria Ground in June 1936, turning professional in January 1939. He developed quickly and was all set to make his senior debut when World War Two broke out and put an end to competitive League football for seven years.

Neil continued to play throughout the hostilities and amassed almost 200 first-team appearances for Stoke, as well as representing England in 10 wartime internationals.

When peacetime soccer resumed in August 1946 Neil was generally regarded as the country's best centre-half, and he went on to make 162 League and FA Cup appearances for the Potters while also winning 27 full England caps, starring in one B international and representing the Football League on five occasions.

An excellent header of the ball, with expert positional sense and a positive tackle, Neil became the king-pin in defence for the Potters and England. Master of all pivotal aspects, he was unyielding, never gave up a lost cause, rarely committed a serious foul and without doubt deserves to be in this book of Stoke City legends.

By May 1950, however, he was ready to leave the Victoria Ground, stating that he was unhappy with the £20-a-week maximum wage limit imposed by the FA and that the local air was not conducive to healthy living, as the nearby pottery kilns continually belched out thick smoke and fumes. He wanted to move his family to a cleaner climate, but what no one envisaged was that this would mean not just switching to another club in England (or Great Britain) but to another continent!

At the end of the 1949–50 season, Neil broke his contract with Stoke and, along with his teammate George Mountford and a handful of other English players, left the country for Colombia to sign for Independienté Santa Fé of Bogotá. He was rewarded with a £5,000–a-year contract, including a £35 match win bonus – a small fortune in those days.

However, Colombia was outside the jurisdiction of the Football Association and its FA was considered a rebel authority. The situation was further aggravated when Neil, who had just won his 27th consecutive England cap, declined to join the squad for the 1950 World Cup Finals in Brazil. Political and social unrest in Colombia made it hard for Neil and his family to settle, and they returned to England after just four weeks.

A suspension from League football followed and he never played for Stoke or England again. He moved to Hull City in February 1951 for £22,500, signed by his former England colleague Raich Carter, who had always admired Neil's skills as a defender. It was also a sad end to a brilliant England career. Neil underwent a knee operation early in the 1952–53 season and never really regained full fitness.

On leaving the Tigers in February 1956, he signed for Crewe Alexandra for £1,250. He switched from Gresty Road to Stockport in October 1957 for the same fee and served Macclesfield Town, albeit briefly, in 1958 before linking up with Wellington Town as player-coach in July 1959.

A year later he joined GKN Sankey's (Wellington) as player-manager and finally hung up his boots in December 1962, aged 40. A decent spell as a coach to Apoel, Cyprus, (from February 1963) preceded his return to England as manager of Colchester United (November 1963). He had mixed fortunes at Layer Road: after relegation from the Third Division in 1965, the club bounced straight back the following season, gaining promotion in fourth place. Unfortunately, he was sacked in May 1968 after another relegation campaign.

Neil scored seven goals in his career – three in wartime football for the Potters and four, all headers, in the Third Division North for Crewe. He made over 550 appearances as a professional, 323 of them in the Football League. Neil later became a licensee, taking over his first pub in Oswaldtwistle and subsequently acting as mine host at the Dog and Doublet in Sandon, Staffordshire.

Ricardo Fuller

Born: 31 October 1979, Kingston, Jamaica

Stoke City record:

Appearances: League 64+8, FA Cup 3+1
Goals: League 25, FA Cup 1
Debut: League, 23 September 2006 v Wolverhampton Wanderers (a)
                   lost 2–0

Also played for: Tivoli Gardens FC (Jamaica), Crystal Palace, West Bromwich
                   Albion (trial), Heart of Midlothian, Preston North End, Portsmouth,
                   Southampton, Ipswich Town and Jamaica (33 full caps)

Ricardo Dwayne Fuller started playing football as a 12-year-old for Jamaican club Tivoli Gardens. He had a trial for Crystal Palace in January 2001 and impressed, signing for the London club for £1 million the following month. Due to tedious knee problems, which resulted in the fans nicknaming him 'Glass Knees', he played just eight games for Palace before returning to Tivoli at the end of the season.

After a fortnight's trial with West Bromwich Albion, Ricardo spent the whole of 2001–02 on loan at Scottish club Hearts, scoring 10 goals in 29 appearances. With Hearts unable to afford to sign him on a permanent basis, Fuller moved to Preston North End for £500,000 in July 2002.

Standing 6ft 3in tall and weighing 13st 3lbs, Ricardo was an imposing figure, and he scored on his senior debut for North End against his old club Crystal Palace. He became a fixture in the Eagles team, grabbing plenty of goals (11 in 20 outings). Unfortunately, he suffered knee ligament damage in early December 2002, which signalled the end of the season for Fuller.

Fuller was still struggling with knee problems during the 2003–04 season, but he still managed to score 19 goals and was in magnificent form at the start of the season, at one point bagging six goals in five games. His performances attracted the likes of Leeds United and Portsmouth, but a failed medical caused Leeds to pull out of a proposed deal.

Portsmouth manager Harry Redknapp was still interested but wary of Fuller's recurring injury problems, so to minimise risk he signed Ricardo on a 'pay-as-you-play' deal, meaning that the club would not lose much money should his knee injuries keep him out of action for any length of time. The £200,000 transfer in August 2004 seemed like a bargain for a player who had fired in 31 goals in 63 appearances for Preston. Unfortunately, he could not carry this form into the Premier League, scoring just one solitary goal in 37 games. He eventually switched to neighbours Southampton in August 2005 for a fee of £90,000, signed by his former manager Harry Redknapp, who had joined Saints eight months earlier.

Ricardo started off quite well at Southampton, but because of his previous connections with Portsmouth he received a considerable amount of abuse from large sections of the Southampton crowd. This unsettled him, and in February 2006 he joined Ipswich Town on loan. He had an eventful time at Portman Road, netting twice in four games while also collecting two yellow cards and one red, the latter against his former club Crystal Palace. His spell at Ipswich came to an end and upon his return to Southampton he was quickly transferred to Stoke City for £500,000 – and what an excellent two years he's had with the Potters.

Fuller made an immediate impact in his first season at the Britannia Stadium and finished up as the club's top scorer with 11 goals. His discipline was an issue, however, and he ended up accumulating two red and 10 yellow cards. The following season was just as good in terms of scoring goals. Indeed, in 2007–08 Ricardo weighed in with a total of 15 in League and Cup matches, including a smartly executed hat-trick in a 3–1 home League win over promotion rivals West Bromwich Albion. He managed to control his discipline, became a huge favourite with the fans and formed a terrific partnership up front with Mama Sidibe as the Potters charged into the Premiership. His pace and strength caused defenders all sorts of problems and his form throughout the campaign earned him a place in the Championship's team of the season.

Ricardo was a member of the Jamaican national squad for seven years (2000–07), during which time he scored four goals in 33 full internationals.

Jimmy Greenhoff

Born: 19 June 1946, Barnsley, Yorkshire

Stoke City record:
Appearances: League 274, FA Cup 26, League Cup 29, others 9
Goals: League 76, FA Cup 11, League Cup 9, others 1
Stoke debut: League, 9 August 1969 v Wolverhampton Wanderers (a) lost
                  3–1

Also played for: Leeds United, Birmingham City, Manchester United, Crewe
                   Alexandra, Toronto Blizzard (NASL), Rochdale, Port Vale,
                   England (1 B and 5 Under-23 caps).
Managed: Rochdale, Port Vale

Jimmy Greenhoff scored in two FA Cup semi-finals for different clubs on the same ground (Goodison Park). His first strike was for Stoke City against Arsenal in 1972 and his second was for Manchester United against Liverpool seven years later. He also netted in another semi-final for Manchester United versus his former club Leeds United at Hillsborough in 1977. He then went on to claim United's fortuitous winner in that year's Final against Liverpool, when a shot from Stoke's future manager Lou Macari bounced off his body and past stranded 'keeper Ray Clemence.

Jimmy returned to Wembley two years later, but this time he had to settle for a runners'-up medal when Arsenal pipped United 3–2 with a last-minute goal from Alan Sunderland.

Previously a League Cup and Inter-Cities Fairs Cup winner with Leeds, and a runner-up in the latter competition with the same club, Jimmy helped Stoke beat Chelsea 2–1 in the 1972 League Cup Final. He also represented the Football League, played once for England's B and turned out five times for the Under-23 side but a full cap eluded him, despite his consistent performances and being rated as one of his country's finest strikers.

Jimmy was a class player – a quality inside-forward, adept at screening the ball with his back to goal and with a defender close on his heels. He was a very clever footballer, highly talented, strong in the air and blessed with a tremendous right-foot shot. He scored some cracking goals in his time, some of them sweetly struck volleys from just inside or outside the penalty-area.

A Yorkshireman, and the brother of Brian, who also played for Leeds and Manchester United, Jimmy helped Barnsley and Yorkshire Boys win the English Schools Trophy before becoming an apprentice at Elland Road in 1961 and turning professional in August 1963. Unable to command a regular place in the Leeds first team, Jimmy was transferred to Birmingham City for £70,000 in August 1968, signed by manager Stan Cullis in the middle of Leeds United's two-legged Fairs Cup Final against Ferencvaros. He scored on his debut for the Blues and went on to claim 11 goals in his first 10 League outings, including a brilliant four-timer and a missed penalty against Fulham in October 1968 as Blues won a thrilling contest 5–4.

Unfortunately for Jimmy, the local and national press as well as local gossip soon made it apparent that Second Division Blues would not be able to retain his services and after spending just 12 months at St Andrews he was sold to Stoke City for £100,000 in August 1969, in a deal clouded in mystery.

He went on to score 97 goals in 338 games for the Potters, including the goal of the season against his former club Birmingham at St Andrew's shortly after he had joined Stoke. He later added 36 more to his tally in 122 outings for Manchester United (November 1976–December 1980) before dropping down the League ladder, playing for Crewe Alexandra until May 1984 then spending a few months as player-manager at Gresty Road.

He then tried his luck in the NASL with Toronto Blizzard (from March 1981), joined Port Vale in August 1981 and became player-manager of Rochdale in March 1983. He returned to Vale Park in the same capacity in May 1984 and later took over as head coach. He eventually quit competitive football in the summer of 1985 to concentrate on coaching youngsters at holiday camps, which he combined with his main job as an insurance broker, based in Stoke-on-Trent.

Jimmy later developed his own business, Greenhoff Peutz and Co, based in Audley, Staffordshire, and he also worked briefly for a Staffordshire paint company.

Andy Griffin

Born:	7 March 1979, Billinge Higher End, Wigan

Stoke City record:

Appearances:	League 99+6, FA Cup 2, League Cup 4+1
Goals:	League 4
Debut:	League, 26 October 1996 as a substitute v Portsmouth (h) won 3-1
Also played for:	Newcastle United, Portsmouth, Derby County, England (Under-18 and 3 Under-21 caps)

When Stoke were promoted to the top flight of English football in May 2008, full-back Andy Griffin became the first Stoke City player to captain the team to promotion to the Premiership, and during the course of the season he reached the milestones of 100 League appearances for the Potters and 300 club and international appearances in his career.

Andy joined Stoke as an apprentice in the spring of 1995 and turned professional in September 1996, having already established a reputation as a solid full-back who was not afraid to go forward. A month later, aged 17, he made his League debut as a second-half substitute against one of his future clubs, Portsmouth, before 10,259 spectators at the Victoria Ground. He played well, and after coming off the bench in the next five games, including an outing against Arsenal at Highbury in a League Cup replay, he established himself in the left-back position at the expense of Northern Ireland international Nigel Worthington. His efforts earned him England Youth recognition, and he ended his first season as a Stoke City regular with 36 appearances under his belt. He also struck his first-ever goal, a cracking left-footer in a 3–1 home victory over Grimsby Town, despite being predominantly right-footed.

Andy's impressive all-round performances quickly attracted the attention of several top-line clubs, including Newcastle United, whose manager at the time was Kenny Dalglish. After making a further 28 appearances for the Potters, and netting another League goal at Huddersfield, Andy eventually moved to St James' Park for £1.5 million in January 1998. At that time it must be said that Stoke were strapped for cash following the building of the club's new Britannia Stadium, and it was no real surprise when Andy left for pastures new. He settled quickly into the Magpies' side, earning further call-ups to the England Youth side as well as gaining the first of three Under-21 caps when he started against Hungary in April 1999.

Unfortunately, in the five seasons from 1998 Andy suffered his fair share of injuries, including damage to both knees, an elbow, his left ankle and his right groin. He also had a hernia operation and suffered a stress fracture of the lower spine, although amazingly he was fit enough to play in the 1999 FA Cup Final defeat to Arsenal. A fighter to the last, he managed to get his playing career back on track with the help of manager Sir Bobby Robson, and he produced several fine performances in 2002–03, culminating in the Champions League encounter against Juventus in which he scored a stunning goal.

However, Andy encountered more injury problems in the 2003–04 season and it was for this reason, as well as the increasing competition for places in the Newcastle side, that his contract was allowed to expire at the end of the season, and he subsequently moved to Portsmouth on a free transfer. Initially, he found himself under fire from the Pompey supporters, but he gradually won them over with his tough-tackling and committed style. Even so, come the end of 2005–06 he was no longer part of Harry Redknapp's plans.

In September of that year he returned to Stoke City on loan. He was immediately welcomed home by the fans, and he soon had them chanting his name after scoring a wonderful 35-yard goal in the fog against Coventry City. In an unfortunate training accident, a rash challenge from Mickey Parker left Andy with a broken third metatarsal and damaged cruciate ligaments in his left knee. On recovering he extended his loan spell at the Britannia Stadium until June 2007, but then, to many fans' surprise, he signed for Derby County on a three-year deal.

However, his stay at Pride Park was short-lived, and in January 2008 Andy returned to Stoke City, with boss Tony Pulis paying £300,000 for his signature. Agreeing a four-and-a-half-year deal, Andy was handed the number-two shirt, and he took over the captain's role after just three weeks when John Eustace joined Watford. Griffin took to the role straight away and was an inspirational leader, instrumental in helping Stoke City return to English football's top tier for the first time since 1985.

Dennis Herod

Born: 27 October 1923, Basford, Staffs

Stoke City record:
Appearances: League 191, FA Cup 24, wartime 125
Goals: League 1
Debut: Southern Regional League, 28 December 1940 v Walsall (a) lost
                 5–1
                 FA Cup, 5 January 1946 v Burnley (h) won 3–1
                 League, 31 August 1946 v Charlton Athletic (h) drew 2–2

Also played for: Trent Vale United, Stockport County, Newcastle Town

Dennis Herod was rather small and light for a goalkeeper, standing 5ft 9in tall and weighing 10st 6lb. Yet he was brave, popular and confident and often dived at the feet of an opponent or stretched full length to turn a shot over the crossbar or round a post.

One of a bevy of talented young 'keepers to emerge on the scene during World War Two, Dennis was recruited by Stoke City as a junior in April 1940, having spent three years playing for Trent Vale United. He was called into the first team for his debut three days after Christmas 1940, but did not have the greatest of matches, the Potters crashing to a 5–1 defeat. Things got even worse for young Dennis when he let in 11 more goals in his next two matches.

Thankfully it was not all doom and gloom as he went on to play in 133 games, including eight FA Cup encounters, during the hostilities. An ever present in 1941–42, he conceded double figures for the first time in his career as the Potters were thrashed 10–0 by Northampton Town, let in nine (three and six) in successive games against West Bromwich Albion and 12 in four clashes with Chester.

The following season he shared the number-one spot with Bates, Bilton, Foster and Sherrett; in 1943–44 he made only one appearance; and in 1944–45 he played in half of the games. He made the position his own once again in 1945–46 when Stoke were on the receiving end of some heavy defeats, including a 9–1 drubbing at Newcastle, a 6–1 reverse at Everton, a 5–1 debacle at Blackburn and 5–2 loss at Manchester City. Dennis also conceded four goals in a game on four occasions.

When League football resumed in August 1946, Dennis was still first choice for the Potters but suffered an injury in the third match and was replaced by Manny Foster and then by Arthur Jepson. Returning to the side in March 1947, Dennis conceded only eight goals in 11 games as the Potters narrowly missed winning the First Division Championship.

Retaining his position throughout 1947–48 and also 1948–49, missing only one League game in each of those campaigns, Dennis had Norman Wilkinson in the wings in 1949–50, and in fact Wilkinson ended the season as Stoke's number-one. But Dennis was back in favour the following term, making 35 League appearances and adding 29 more to his tally in 1951–52, as well as having the pleasure of scoring the only goal of his senior professional career.

It came in the away First Division encounter with Aston Villa in mid-February. Injured while thwarting a Villa attack, he pushed out to the wing, simply to cause the home side as much trouble as possible. He did more than that – he scored the winning goal in a 3–2 victory.

Back between the posts for the next match, Dennis continued to perform well before finally giving way to the former Chelsea 'keeper Bill Robertson, who was signed from Birmingham City. Dennis deputised for Robertson in 12 games that season. He played in the reserves prior to leaving the Victoria Ground for Stockport County in July 1953 for a fee of £750.

Dennis appeared in 340 League, FA Cup and wartime matches in 13 years with the Potters and kept 56 clean sheets in his 215 senior outings. He spent two seasons at Edgeley Park, during which time he added another 37 senior appearances to his career tally. Retiring in May 1955, Dennis later ventured into the greengrocery business and occasionally turned out (in an emergency) for his adopted team, Newcastle Town. He will soon be celebrating his 85th birthday, making him one of the oldest former Stoke City players still with us today.

Tom Holford

Born: 28 January 1878, Hanley, Stoke-on-Trent
Died: 6 April 1964, Blurton, Stoke-on-Trent

Stoke City record:
Appearances: League 248, FA Cup 21
Goals: League 30, FA Cup 3
Debut: League, 17 September 1898 v Sheffield United (a) drew 1–1

Also played for: Granville's Night School (Stoke), Cobridge, Manchester City, Port
                 Vale (player-manager), England (1 full cap)

Nicknamed 'Dirty Tommy' for his sometimes reckless and careless tackling, Tom Holford was a cousin of the former Stoke City centre-forward Wilf Kirkham and played for Granville's Night School and Cobridge before joining Stoke as a full-time professional in May 1898.

He made an impressive League debut in a 1–1 draw away to Sheffield United and was the cornerstone of the Potters' defence for seven full seasons from 1901 to 1908. In all, he accumulated 269 senior appearances and scored 33 goals for the Potters, being an ever present two years running (1903–05) and missing only six games in five seasons.

His name was first on the team sheet and he certainly gave the Potters grand service with his solid, all-action, determined and robust performances. A pugnacious footballer, he never shirked a tackle, covered acres of ground during every game and above all was blessed with a never-say-die attitude and a will to win.

In fact, it took Tom three seasons before he really established himself as a regular in the Stoke line up. But once in, he stayed, and would play in a variety of positions, never criticising his manager for playing him where he did not really want to be. He simply loved playing football and was confident enough to occupy any given position. He even took over in goal in an emergency.

Standing only 5ft 5in tall and weighing barely 9st, he was amazingly strong and loved to battle it out with taller and far stronger opponents. He was capped by England against Ireland at Molineux in 1903 when he deputised for Frank Forman and played a fine game in a 4–0 win. This was his only representative honour, though he deserved more.

Tom was a great favourite with the Stoke supporters and it came as a huge shock when he chose to leave the club in 1908 for Manchester City, with whom he won a Second Division Championship medal in 1910, scoring 12 goals from the centre-forward position. He netted 38 times in 184 outings for City up to May 1914, when he left Manchester to become Port Vale's player-manager.

A key member of the Valiants side that won the North Staffs Infirmary Cup a year later, Tom was then conscripted into the forces in the summer of 1917. He served with the Royal Artillery and appeared as a guest for Nottingham Forest during World War One (season 1918–19) before returning to Vale for the start of the 1919–20 campaign. He continued to play for Vale on a regular basis and added a Staffordshire Cup and two more Infirmary Cup-winners' medals to his collection before retiring to become the club's trainer in April 1922.

Still keeping himself fit, he was asked in an emergency to turn out in two Football League matches, both against Derby County, on 29 March and 5 April 1924. When he played in the second fixture at The Baseball Ground, he was aged 46 years and 68 days, the oldest player ever to star for Port Vale and now the sixth-oldest player ever to appear in a competitive League game in England.

He was Port Vale's trainer for eight seasons before taking over as the club's full-time manager in June 1932, but he was relieved of his duties in September 1935 so that he could act as the club's senior scout, continuing in this field until 1950. He also acted as the club's trainer during World War Two, from July 1939 until July 1946, and all told Tom was associated with the Valiants for 36 years.

Alan Hudson

Born: 21 June 1931, Chelsea, London

Stoke City record:
Appearances: League 143+1, FA Cup 8, League Cup 8, others 2
Goals: League 9
Debut: League, 19 January 1974 v Liverpool (h) drew 1–1

Also played for: Fulham (Schoolboy), Chelsea, Arsenal, Seattle Sounders (NASL),
                    Hercules CF (Alicante, Spain), England (2 full caps)

Alan Hudson was one of the most naturally gifted midfielders of his generation, a skilful and natural playmaker with tremendous vision and comfortable using either foot, yet his career was marred by controversies and injury problems. World Cup-winning England captain Bobby Moore once said of him 'Alan could have conquered the world, but there was no guarantee he was going to conquer his temperament.'

Born and brought up near the King's Road, Alan was rejected by Fulham as a Schoolboy before signing for Chelsea Juniors. Injury denied him the chance to become the Blues' youngest-ever player at the age of 16 and he eventually made his senior debut nine months later in a 5-0 hammering at Southampton on 1 February 1969.

Alan found himself in a Chelsea side noted for its flair and skill, complete with equally flamboyant footballers such as Peter Osgood and Charlie Cooke. It was during the 1969–70 season that he established himself as the team's playmaker, creating plenty of goal chances for his colleagues as Chelsea finished third in the First Division.

He played in every match in Chelsea's run to the FA Cup Final in 1970, but missed the Final itself due to another injury. He did, however, play a major role in Chelsea's replayed European Cup-Winners' Cup Final victory over Real Madrid in Athens a year later.

The debt burden caused by the building of the then new East Stand at Stamford Bridge forced Chelsea to sell some key players, and after defeat to Stoke City in the 1972 League Cup Final, and a bust-up with manager Dave Sexton, Alan was placed on the transfer list (with others) in January 1974. Within a month he had joined Stoke City for £240,000, making his debut for the Potters in a 1–1 draw with Liverpool when he starred alongside Geoff Hurst (the goalscorer) and Jimmy Greenhoff.

Stoke manager Tony Waddington saw Alan as the final piece of the jigsaw that would turn the Potters into genuine Championship challengers in 1975. He played some of the best football of his career under Waddington's shrewd leadership as Stoke finished just four points away from eventual champions Derby County in his first season at the Victoria Ground.

Owing to a ban from international football after refusing to tour with the England Under-23 side, Alan did not make his England debut until 1975, when sparkling performances earned him two call-ups from England chief Don Revie. He starred when the World Champions West Germany were beaten 2–0 at Wembley and again in the 5–0 thumping of Cyprus. However, injuries and clashes with Revie meant that those two caps were the only ones he gained.

Financial troubles at Stoke forced Alan's sale to Arsenal in December 1976 for £200,000. He helped the Gunners reach the 1978 FA Cup Final, which they lost 1–0 to Ipswich Town, but differences with the Arsenal manager Terry Neill meant that he moved to Seattle Sounders for £100,000 at the age of 27. Alan subsequently played for Hércules CF in Spain before returning to Second Division Chelsea in August 1983, although illness and injury denied him the chance to play for them again. There was also a nostalgic return to Stoke, where he helped the club avoid relegation from the old First Division in the 1983–84 season.

Since his retirement in May 1985, Alan has had mixed fortunes in business and in health. He opened a nightclub (albeit only briefly) in Stoke, penned a column for the *Sporting Life*, had problems with alcoholism, was declared bankrupt, and in 1997 sustained serious injuries in a car crash which saw him spend around two months in a coma. After this setback he was not expected to walk again, but thankfully he managed to make a recovery.

In June 2006, he teamed up with Radio Napa in Cyprus and reported on the FIFA World Cup in Germany.

Sir Geoff Hurst, MBE

Born: 8 December 1941, Ashton-under-Lyne

Stoke City record:
Appearances: League 103+5, FA Cup 3, League Cup 10, others 9
Goals: League 30, League Cup 6, others 3
Debut: League, 12 August 1972 v Crystal Palace (h) won 2–0

Also played for: Halstead FC, Chelmsford City, West Ham United, Cape Town
                Spurs, West Bromwich Albion, Cork Celtic, Seattle Sounders, Al-
                Kuwait, Telford United (player-manager), England (4 Under-23
                and 49 full caps)
Managed: Chelsea

Geoff Hurst stands unique as the only man to have scored a hat-trick in a World Cup Final, doing so for the winners England against West Germany at Wembley in 1966.

Starting out as a wing-half for his school team (King's Road Secondary Modern) and playing in that same position for Halstead FC and Chelmsford City, he joined West Ham United as an amateur in July 1957 and turned professional in April 1959 after gaining England Youth honours. By sheer determination and hard work, he developed quickly and after being switched into the forward line by Hammers manager Ron Greenwood he became one of the finest goalscorers in world football, respected by his fellow professionals for his unselfish ability to create as well as take chances with both feet and his head.

Geoff made his League debut against the FA Cup holders Nottingham Forest in February 1960, and in the 12 years up to 1972 he scored 252 goals in 502 senior appearances for West Ham, 180 of them coming in 411 League games. In 1968 he netted a double hat-trick in an 8–0 home League victory over Sunderland.

He helped the Hammers win the FA Cup in 1964 (against Preston) and the European Cup-Winners' Cup the following year (against 1860 Munich), with both matches at Wembley. He then made it a remarkable hat-trick of Cup Final triumphs when he helped England lift the Jules Rimet trophy for the first time, his second goal being regarded as one of the most controversial in World Cup history as his shot hit the crossbar and appeared not to land over the line.

He also played in the losing League Cup Final of 1966 (against his future club West Bromwich Albion), and the following season he won the treble of the First Division, the FA Cup and the League Cup.

Geoff had made his full international debut against West Germany only five months before the World Cup and it was an injury to Jimmy Greaves that got him into the side. He scored the winning goal against Argentina in the quarter-final, played his part in the semi-final victory over Portugal and then created history in the Final itself. He went on to appear in the 1970 World Cup Finals in Mexico and ended up with 49 full caps and 24 goals.

In June 1972 he moved to Stoke City for a fee of £80,000. He served the Potters exceptionally well for

three years, amassing a fine record of 39 goals in 129 competitive matches. He netted 13 times in his first season at the Victoria Ground when playing alongside Jimmy Greenhoff and John Ritchie, and after a summer loan spell with Cape Town Spurs in South Africa he was leading marksman with 15 goals in 1973–74 and weighed in with 11 more in 1974–75.

In August 1975 Geoff moved to West Bromwich Albion for £20,000 (signed by Johnny Giles). He spent just over six months at The Hawthorns before transferring to Cork Celtic, later assisting Seattle Sounders and then Telford United (as player-manager). Over a period of five years (1977–82) he was assistant coach to the England team, taking up a similar position with Chelsea during that time. In fact, he was appointed manager at Stamford Bridge in September 1979 but quit in April 1981. He later played for Al-Kuwait and also coached the England Under-21 side for a short time. After leaving football, Geoff became a publican at Whitmore before accepting a directorship in a motor insurance company (Motorplan) and later becoming a director of McDonald's.

His playing career realised 296 goals in 716 competitive matches, and he also played in one county cricket match for Essex against Lancashire in 1962, being bowled out for a duck by Peter Hilton. He was awarded the MBE in 1975 and a knighthood in 1998.

Geoff's father, Charles, played football for Oldham Athletic, Bristol Rovers and Rochdale.

Joe Johnson

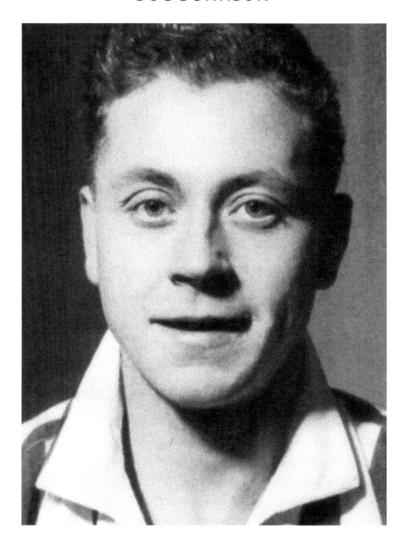

Born: 4 April 1911, Grimsby
Died: 8 August 1983, West Bromwich

Stoke City record:
Appearances: League 184, FA Cup 9
Goals: League 54, FA Cup 3
Debut: League, 7 May 1937 v Bradford Park Avenue (h) won 1–0.

Also played for: Cleethorpes Royal Saints, Scunthorpe & Lindsey United, Bristol
City, (wartime guest for Crewe Alexandra, Leicester City, Notts
County), West Bromwich Albion, Hereford United, Northwich
Victoria, England (5 full caps)

In their book *A Century of English International Football 1872–1972*, Morley Farror and Douglas Lamming described Joe Johnson as being 'an excellent little winger who achieved a good scoring record for a left-winger. Possibly the highlight of his career was the 1937 Scotland match when his skilful, swerving runs bemused the Scots defence.'

Stoke City supporter Wade Martin wrote in his *Master Potters* series 'Joe was noted for his penetrating and swerving runs and with Stanley Matthews on the right and Joe on the left, Freddie Steele certainly had the very best of service.'

In my book *The A-Z of Stoke City*, I stated that Joe was 'a fine player who loved to start his runs deep in his own half of the field. He often cut in fast to shoot at goal.'

Those three comments sum Joe Johnson up to a tee. He was a splendid footballer whose statistics would have been a lot better if World War Two had not materialised when it did.

Joe's first job on leaving school was with a fishmonger and at weekends he played football for Cleethorpes Royal Saints, whom he joined initially in July 1926. After some enterprising displays on the left wing he was approached and subsequently signed by Scunthorpe & Lindsey United, then a Midland League club. Registered as a professional in April 1928, he spent three seasons with the 'Iron' before transferring to Bristol City for £1,200 in May 1931.

He made only eight appearances for the Ashton Gate club who, at the time, were in serious financial difficulties. As a result, in April 1932, after Stoke had drawn 0–0 with Bristol City, the home directors informed Stoke's manager Tom Mather that he could have the pick of any of his players. After a meeting with his own directors, it was agreed that Tom should sign Joe, for what was to prove a bargain fee of just £2,500. He made his debut for the Potters on the last day of that season against Bradford Park Avenue, when goalkeeper Roy John and Joe Buller also made their first appearances for the club.

Joe missed only one game in 1932–33, scoring 15 League goals and helping the Potters win the Second Division Championship.

The following season he did not score as many goals but was just as effective down the left wing, and in 1934–35 he was second-top scorer with 11 goals, behind hot-shot centre-forward Tommy Sale.

After another decent season when he had to battle against a tedious leg injury, Joe regained full fitness and in November 1936 was selected for England against Ireland on his home patch, the Victoria Ground, in front of a near 48,000 crowd. Fellow 'Stokie' Freddie Steele had replaced Sale, and led the England line that day in a 3–1 win.

Joe missed the next international against Hungary but was back on the left wing for the big one against Scotland at Hampden Park in April 1937 in front of a near 150,000 crowd. He was on the losing side this time but did well enough to gain three more caps in comprehensive victories over Norway (6–0), Sweden (4–0) and Finland (8–0), scoring in each of the last two.

Six months after winning his last cap and having scored 57 goals in 194 appearances for the Potters, Joe was transferred to West Bromwich Albion for £6,500 in November 1937. Although the Baggies were relegated to the Second Division, he stayed at The Hawthorns for eight and a half years, guesting for three other clubs during the hostilities. With his wartime record added, he hit 45 goals in 145 games for Albion before moving to Hereford United on a free transfer in May 1946.

Later with Northwich Victoria, Joe announced his retirement in May 1950 and returned to West Bromwich, where he ran a café in Dartmouth Park, not too far away from The Hawthorns, for many years.

Graham Kavanagh

Born: 2 December 1973, Dublin

Stoke City record:
Appearances: League 198+8, FA Cup 6, League Cup 16+2, others 15
Goals: League 35, League Cup 7, others 4
Debut: League, 14 September 1996 (sub) v Birmingham City (a) lost
                3–1

Also played for: Home Farm, Middlesbrough, Darlington, Stoke City, Cardiff City,
                Wigan Athletic, Sunderland, Sheffield Wednesday, Republic of
                Ireland (Schoolboy, Youth, 1 B, 9 Under-21 and 16 full caps)

Graham Kavanagh is appreciated throughout the Leagues for his hard but fair tackling and the creative dimension in his play. Nicknamed the 'Silver Fox', he started out as a positive and very effective inside-forward (an attacking midfielder), but as the years went by he switched his priorities to become a holding player in front of the back four.

He moved into the Football League (from Home Farm) in 1991 when he joined Middlesbrough. He went on to appear in 47 senior games for the Teesside club, and after a loan spell with Darlington he switched his allegiance to Stoke City in September 1996, signed by manager Lou Macari for £250,000.

He went straight into the Potters' midfield, accompanying Gerry McMahon and Kevin Keen in the engine room. He had a decent enough first season, making over 40 appearances as the Potters finished in mid-table in Division One.

During 1997–98 Graham was clearly upset by the reaction of the Stoke fans as the team stuttered along during the second half of the campaign but he put that to one side and battled on with grim determination in the middle of the park in a bold effort to improve results.

He took over as Stoke's penalty taker and indeed dead ball expert, and he scored two cracking goals in a 4–0 League Cup win over Burnley. He also added to his international CV by representing the Republic of Ireland at B team and senior levels, having previously appeared in his country's Schoolboy, Youth and Under-21 sides. He would go from strength to strength on the international front, eventually taking his senior tally of caps to 16 and his Under-21 tally to nine, despite being an exile for four and a half years, from May 1999 to November 2003.

His last senior cap was gained in August 2003 against Holland.

After making almost 250 League and Cup appearances for the Potters and gaining an Auto Windscreens Shield-winner's medal in 2000 when he scored in a 2–1 victory over Bristol City at Wembley Stadium, Graham left the Britannia Stadium for Cardiff City in a £1 million deal in July 2001 – good, solid business by the Potters, who made a healthy £750,000 profit!

Graham continued to impress in midfield for the Bluebirds and over a period of almost four years amassed a further 165 first-class appearances and 31 goals before transferring to Wigan Athletic for £395,000 in March 2005, a move that he did not really want but to which the Welsh club agreed because of financial difficulties.

Seventeen months and 55 outings later, Graham chose to leave the JJB Stadium to try his luck on Wearside, signing for his fellow countryman Roy Keane's Sunderland for £500,000. He agreed a three-year contract but unfortunately injuries curtailed his first season at the Stadium of Light, and Graham underwent two knee operations. He did, however, play in enough games (14) to receive a Championship medal.

Exactly a year on and after regaining full fitness, Graham was linked with a transfer deadline day move to Leeds United, but the move failed to materialise. However, 48 hours later, on 2 September, the *Sunday People* newspaper linked Graham with a possible loan move to Elland Road along with fellow Sunderland player Roy O'Donovan. Nothing happened in this direction either and he subsequently joined Sheffield Wednesday in an emergency one-month loan deal. He then went out and scored his first goal for the Owls against Watford shortly afterwards. He had a second loan spell at Hillsborough in 2008.

Graham, who is not getting any younger but is still reasonably fit and willing, has now accumulated a career record of more than 575 club and international appearances and scored over 80 goals.

Kevin Keen

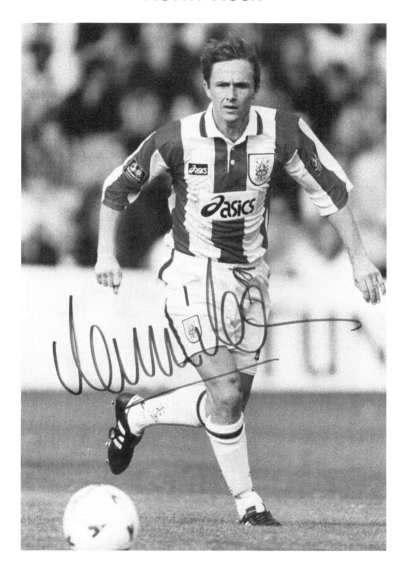

Born: 25 February 1967, Amersham

Stoke City record:
Appearances: League 147+30, FA Cup 6, League Cup 13+3, others 3+1
Goals: League 10, League Cup 2
Debut: League, 22 October 1994 v Oldham Athletic (a) drew 0–0

Also played for: Wycombe Wanderers, West Ham United (2 spells, also caretaker
                 manager), Wolverhampton Wanderers, Macclesfield Town (also
                 manager), England (Schoolboy and Youth caps)

Kevin Keen is the son of former professional Mike Keen, who played in midfield for Luton Town, Watford and Queen's Park Rangers, lifting the Football League Cup at Wembley with QPR in 1967.

Kevin was a member of the High Wycombe Under-15 team that won the English Schools Trophy in 1981, and he gained several England schoolboy caps as well as becoming the youngest ever player to appear in a first-team game for Southern League side Wycombe Wanderers, making his debut at the age of 15 years and 209 days in September 1982.

He played three games for Wycombe before joining West Ham United as a 16-year-old apprentice in 1983 and signed professional forms a year later in March 1984. He helped the Hammers reserve side win the Combination League and collected 15 England Youth caps. He made his first appearance for the Londoners as a substitute in a 5–2 home League defeat by Liverpool in September 1986.

He continued to serve West Ham until the summer of 1993, playing in a total of 279 senior games and netting 30 goals. Keen twice helped the Hammers reach the League Cup semi-final and also the FA Cup semi-final, finishing up a loser each time. He suffered two relegation campaigns (1989 and 1993) and his final game for the London club came in a 2–0 home win over Cambridge United in May 1993, which clinched promotion to the newly created Premiership. Soon afterwards, a dispute over a new contract saw Kevin drop down a division and join Wolverhampton Wanderers for £600,000. After making 54 appearances in the 1993–94 season he was on the move again, this time linking up with his former manager at Upton Park, Lou Macari now at Stoke City.

Keen signed for the Potters in October 1994 for £300,000 and served the club exceedingly well, amassing a fine record of a dozen goals in just over 200 senior appearances during his six years at the Victoria Ground. He made his debut at Boundary Park in a goalless draw with Oldham, linking up in midfield with Toddy Orlygsson, Nigel Gleghorn and, later in the season, his old Molineux colleague Keith Downing. He made 21 League appearances in 1994–95, notching two goals, the first against his former club Wolves in a 1–1 stalemate at the Victoria Ground.

In 1995–96 Kevin played in 37 first-class matches but, due to damaged ankle ligaments and then a broken fibula sustained in the away game at Swindon on his return from his first injury, he appeared in only 20 games, 13 as a substitute, the following season. In 1997–98 he started off in superb form, but then a change of manager saw him slip into the reserves before he returned to the senior side when Alan Durban took temporary charge of the team.

After that, Kevin produced some excellent performances on the right side of midfield and at times was the team's outstanding player. In September 2000 he went to Macclesfield Town on a free tranfer.

As a 'Potter', Kevin actually played under seven managers – Macari, Chic Bates, Chris Kamara, Durban, Brian Little, Gary Megson and Gudjon Thordarson.

He later acted as caretaker manager of Macclesfield for a month following Gil Prescott's decision to concentrate on a role as director of football in October 2001. Subsequently released in May 2002 when his contract was not renewed, Kevin immediately returned to West Ham as academy coach, having gained his UEFA A coaching certificate in 2001. Later appointed reserve-team coach, he then took over as first-team coach in October 2006. Then, following the sacking of manager Alan Pardew two months later, he was placed in temporary charge of the Hammers until Alan Curbishley was appointed, at which point Kevin reverted to his previous role as reserve-team coach.

Howard Kendall

Born: 22 May 1946, Ryton-on-Tyne

Stoke City record:
Appearances: League 82, FA Cup 3, League Cup 6
Goals: League 9, League Cup 1
Debut: League, 20 August 1977 v Mansfield Town (a) lost 2–1

Also played for: Preston North End, Everton (2 spells, the second as player-
                  manager), Birmingham City, Blackburn Rovers (player-manager),
                  England (6 Under-23 caps)
Also managed: Everton, Athletic Bilbao (Spain), Manchester City, Xanthi
                  (Greece), Notts County, Sheffield United, Ethnikos Piraeus

Midfielder Howard Kendall rose to prominence when he became the youngest player (at that time) ever to appear in an FA Cup Final, lining up for Preston North End against West Ham in 1964 at the age of 17 years and 345 days – a record he lost to Paul Allen, ironically of West Ham, in 1980.

On 8 May 1981, Howard also became the youngest manager ever appointed by Everton, aged 34 years and 351 days. Voted Manager of the Year for 1984–85 after steering the Merseysiders to the First Division title and winning the European Cup-Winners' Cup, he later added a second League Championship to his list of achievements (1987). Howard also guided the Merseysiders to three successive Charity Shield victories as well as winning the FA Cup in 1984 and finishing runners-up in the same competition in 1985 and 1986.

Described as the 'complete midfielder', Howard represented Ryton & District Schools and played for Wales at Schoolboy level before joining Preston as an apprentice in June 1961, turning professional in May 1963.

Four years later, after making over 100 appearances for North End, he moved to Everton for £80,000 (March 1967) and the following year played in his second FA Cup Final when the Merseysiders lost 1–0 to West Bromwich Albion. He also represented England at Under-23 level against Wales, the first of six caps in this category, although a full cap eluded him. He also played for the Football League.

Howard teamed up with Colin Harvey and Alan Ball in Everton's engine room, becoming a firm favourite with the fans, who later took to him as a manager.

He scored 29 goals in 276 appearances for Everton in seven years, helping them win the League title in 1970 before moving to Birmingham City in March 1974 in a complicated deal involving Bob Latchford and Archie Styles, Everton receiving £350,000 as their share of the three-player transaction.

Appointed captain of Blues, Howard's experience went a long way in helping the club retain its First Division status at the end of the 1973–74 season and the following year he missed only three League games when Blues reached the semi-finals of the FA Cup.

After 134 games for the St Andrew's club, Howard switched to Stoke City for £40,000 in August 1977. He spent two excellent years at the Victoria Ground and made 91 appearances for the Potters, linking up superbly well in midfield with Paul Richardson. He had a splendid first season, being an ever present and scoring seven goals, his first in a 4–0 home League win over Sheffield United. He also netted in the return fixture at Bramall Lane (won 2–1), scored a crucial penalty against Bristol Rovers (won 3–2) and delivered a fine strike in a 2–1 victory at Luton.

In 1978–79 Howard's presence, and certainly his experience, went a long way in helping the Potters gain promotion to the top flight. He missed only two League games and grabbed the winning goal against Preston at Deepdale. Surprisingly, Howard left the Victoria Ground in June 1979 to become player-manager of Blackburn Rovers, signed for £20,000.

After guiding Rovers to the Third Division title in 1980, he returned to his former home, Goodison Park, in the same capacity in May 1981, retiring as a player the following year with a record of 65 goals in 613 League appearances accumulated over 19 years with five clubs.

Howard remained as Everton manager until June 1987 when he took charge of Athletic Bilbao, retaining that position without success until November 1989. A month later he became boss of Manchester City (no joy there either) and in November 1990 returned to Goodison Park for another spell as manager, remaining in office until December 1993. After that he managed Xanthi (May–November 1994), Notts County (January–April 1995), Sheffield United (1995–97), Everton again (1997–98) and Ethnikos Piraeus (1998–99).

Howard's uncle, Harry Taylor, played for Newcastle United in the 1950s.

Johnny King

Born: 9 August 1932, Wrenbury, near Nantwich, Cheshire

Stoke City record:
Appearances: League 284, FA Cup 26, League Cup 1
Goals: League 106, FA Cup 7
Debut: League, 21 September 1953 v Rotherham United (a) drew 2–2

Also played for: Cardiff City, Crewe Alexandra (2 spells)

Johnny King was a short, chunky inside or centre-forward, naturally left-footed with a good, strong shot. He was deceptively quick over 20–30 yards, possessed a neat body-swerve and developed a fine scoring record over a long period of time, netting well over 180 goals in more than 570 first-class matches for three different clubs, including a League record of 172 goals in 548 outings.

Johnny began his career as a junior at Gresty Road in August 1947 and, after two decent seasons in the second team, he turned professional in October 1949. At Crewe he formed a splendid left-wing partnership with Frank Blunstone, who later went on to play outside-left for Chelsea and England.

Johnny remained with the Railwaymen until he joined the Potters for a substantial fee of £8,000 in September 1953, signed by manager Frank Taylor, who pondered hard and long before finalising the deal.

Johnny went straight into the Potters' first team at inside-left, Johnny Sellars dropping out to enable Alan Martin to switch to left-half. He played well in his first game, twice going close to scoring while helping his side earn a point from a 2–2 draw with Rotherham United at Millmoor.

That was the first of 371 senior appearances Johnny made for Stoke and his first goal (of 113) was scored on his home debut five days later, earning his side a point from a 1–1 draw with one of the promotion favourites, Luton Town. Over 24,000 fans turned up, the biggest crowd at the Victoria Ground at that stage in the season.

Johnny ended that season with 12 goals to his credit, and in 1954–55 he netted a total of 20, his best return for the Potters. This haul included two hat-tricks: the first, which contained two penalties, came in the second match, a 3–0 win at Nottingham Forest; and the second in a 3–2 Christmas Day home victory over Bury.

Forming a fine strike partnership with the impressive Frank Bowyer, Johnny continued to tease and torment defenders throughout 1955–56 and bagged another 18 goals, including his third treble for the club, this one in a 4–2 away League win over Doncaster Rovers. Although his personal goal tally dried up somewhat in 1956–57 (only nine goals scored in 35 outings), he did create chances galore for his colleagues, namely Bowyer, flying wingers Tim Coleman and Harry Oscroft, and George Kelly. The Potters rattled in 85 goals that term, 83 of them in the League, which was their highest tally since 1946–47.

Johnny assisted in four of the seven goals that Coleman netted in a comprehensive 8–0 home win over hapless Lincoln City in February, and he scored the other himself. Over the next three seasons Johnny continued to hit the target, claiming 39 goals in 125 games alongside strike partners including the former Wolves and England star Dennis Wilshaw.

It was something of a surprise to the loyal Stoke fans when Johnny was transferred to Cardiff City for £12,000 in May 1961, having joined the list of star players who have scored over a century of first-class goals for the Potters. He finished up with 106 in the League alone, and to this day only Tommy Sale, Freddie Steele, Frank Bowyer and John Ritchie have scored more.

After spending just the one season at Ninian Park (scoring six goals in 33 appearances), Johnny completed a full circle by returning to Crewe Alexandra for a second spell in June 1962. This time round he remained at Gresty Road for five years, becoming one of the Railwaymen's finest-ever players. He helped them win promotion from the Fourth Division in 1963 and also represented the FA while with them. He eventually retired through injury in May 1967, three months short of his 35th birthday.

Away from football, Johnny and his Stoke City teammate George Kelly formed a fine doubles partnership at lawn tennis and at one stage were on the brink of qualifying for the Wimbledon doubles Championship.

John Kirton

Born: 4 March 1916, Aberdeen
Died: 12 March 1996, Stoke-on-Trent

Stoke City record:
Appearances: League 219, FA Cup 30, wartime 55
Goals: League 2
Debut: League, 28 December 1936 v Chelsea (a) lost 1–0

Also played for: St Marcher's FC (Aberdeen), Banks o'Dee, Bradford City, Hinckley Athletic, Downings FC, Scotland (3 Schoolboy caps and 1 wartime cap)

Jock Kirton spent almost 18 years with Stoke City, during which time he appeared in more than 300 first-team matches. If World War Two had not disrupted his career, he could well have gone on to become the Potters' record appearance-maker at senior level.

A splendid wing-half, efficient in every sense of the word, Jock was spotted by manager Bob McGrory's excellent scouting network North of the border. He had already represented his country in a handful of Schoolboy internationals and played for two junior clubs in Scotland, St Marcher's and Banks o'Dee, before joining the Potters as a full-time professional in November 1935 at the age of 19.

However, his opportunities of playing competitive League football were limited during his first three years at the Victoria Ground, owing to the presence and superb form of Arthur Tutin and Frank Soo. Indeed, Jock failed to get a single call-up in 1935–36. He made 14 starts the following season and 12 more in 1937–38 before having a fine pre-war campaign when he starred in 38 senior matches, all at left-half, having taken over from Soo, who was switched to the right in place of Tutin.

Unfortunately, the hostilities began in earnest soon afterwards, and Jock's outings for the Potters were rather spasmodic for seven years. He played when he could and kept himself extremely fit, and as a result was rewarded with a wartime cap by Scotland at Wembley in February 1944, when a crowd of 80,000 saw him play alongside Matt Busby in England's emphatic 6–2 win. However, he had to wait until the 1944–45 season before having a decent spell with the Potters, making 11 consecutive appearances at the end of that campaign, when he played mainly alongside Neil Franklin.

He followed up in 1945–46 with 32 outings, including seven in the FA Cup, being on the pitch at Burden Park for a sixth-round encounter with Bolton when that crowd disaster took place and killed 33 spectators and injured over 500 others. Jock never got over that incident, neither did his teammates.

When the Football League was reintroduced in 1946–47, Stoke had a decent team and were considered by some as potential champions. Jock lined up across the centre of the field with Frank Mountford and Franklin, while Stanley Matthews and Freddie Steele were in the forward line. Jock had a fine season but was disappointed along with his colleagues when the title was lost on the final day, with defeat at Sheffield United.

Full of energy and commitment, Jock, who eventually became team captain, was a tireless competitor with a never-say-die attitude. He was the mainstay of the Potters team for quite a while, although injuries seriously interrupted his performances in 1948–49 and again the following season.

He had an outstanding campaign in 1946–47, when he made 42 appearances and scored his first-ever goal for the club in an excellent 5–2 win over Chelsea at Stamford Bridge when the turnout was 68,189. He had to wait until September 1948 for his second goal, and again it came in a victory, this time 3–2 over Derby County at the Baseball Ground.

At the end of the 1952–53 season Jock left the Victoria Ground to become player-coach of Bradford City. He held that position until March 1954 and made eight appearances for the Valley Parade club before choosing to enter non-League football with Leicestershire-based Hinckley Athletic. Prior to his retirement in May 1960 Jock assisted local side Downings FC, and upon retirement from the game he settled down in his adopted home of Stoke-on-Trent. Jock was 80 when he died in 1996.

Liam Lawrence

Born: 14 December 1981, Retford

Stoke City record:
Appearances: League 67+1, FA Cup 3, League Cup 1
Goals: League 19, FA Cup 1
Debut: 18 November 2006 v Hull City (a) won 2–0

Also played for: Mansfield Town and Sunderland

A strong right-sided midfielder, hard-working, skilful and thrusting, Liam Lawrence celebrated his third promotion to the Premiership in four seasons when he helped Stoke City to glory in 2007–08. Prior to that, he had twice helped Sunderland climb into the top flight, first in 2004–05 and again in 2006–07, when he played in 12 games early in the season before his transfer to the Potters.

An excellent crosser of the ball, whether it be on the run or from a dead-ball situation, Liam broke into League football with Mansfield Town, whom he joined initially as an apprentice in May 1998, turning professional at Field Mill in July 2000 under manager Billy Dearden.

Over the next four years or so, he scored 39 goals in 153 competitive games for the Stags, suffering the disappointment of missing a penalty in the shoot-out at the end of the Third Division Play-off Final against Huddersfield Town. However, within a season of playing at that level, he suddenly found himself in the Premiership with Sunderland, whose manager Mick McCarthy recruited him for just £175,000 in July 2004.

Liam quickly established himself as a fan favourite on Wearside, and he had a pretty good first season at the Stadium of Light, scoring six goals in a total of 32 games. He also helped create Marcus Stewart's crucial goal in a win over fellow promotion candidates Wigan Athletic at the JJB Stadium in early April, a game that effectively clinched the Championship and a place in the Premier League.

Following Sunderland's entry into the big-time with the likes of Arsenal, Chelsea, Liverpool and Manchester United, Liam found it hard to cement his place in the first team for the first few months of the 2005–06 season. During the course of the season he did manage to complete 33 competitive games for the club, scoring three goals, all of them spectacular. The first came in a 2–2 draw with arch-rivals Newcastle United at St James' Park, the second in a 2–1 defeat at Fulham and the third, also in a 2–1 reverse, at home to Chelsea.

Despite Sunderland eventually being relegated with a then record low 15 points, Liam was regarded as one of the better players in a disappointing season for the team and was voted runner-up to Dean Whitehead for Player of the Year.

After signing a four-year contract with Sunderland in August 2006, Liam fell out with manager Roy Keane and returned to Stoke City having played only 13 games for Sunderland during the first half of that season. Initially signed on a two-month loan deal, he agreed a permanent move to the Potters when the transfer window opened in January 2007 and was signed by manager Tony Pulis for what has proved to be a bargain fee of just £500,000.

Liam contributed five League goals during the second half of that season while playing in a total of 28 first-team games for the Potters. The team finished eighth in the Championship, missing out on the Play-offs by just two points after a seven-match unbeaten run had taken them to within striking distance of sixth-placed Southampton. In fact, a win (instead of a draw) at QPR on the last day of the season would have seen the Potters finish above the Saints.

Liam was called up to the Republic of Ireland squad (his grandfather was born in Kerry) in February 2006 for the home friendly match against Sweden the following month. Newly appointed Republic of Ireland manager Steve Staunton brought four young Premiership players into the squad but, sadly for Liam, he only made the subs' bench. He continued to be a regular in Staunton's squads was still awaiting his first cap when Giovanni Trapatonni took over in 2008.

Liam is a very popular player at the Britannia Stadium and won Player of the Year for the 2007–08 season, producing some splendid all-action performances at home and away and playing a major part in Stoke's promotion success. He scored a total of 15 goals (in 44 appearances) during that promotion-winning season, including 14 in the League alone.

Norman Lewis

Born: 13 June 1908, Wolverhampton
Died: c.1972, Wolverhampton

Stoke City record:

Appearances: League 159, FA Cup 11
Debut: League, 28 September 1929 v Bristol City (h) won 6–2

Also played for: Sunbeam Works (Wolverhampton), Wolverhampton Wanderers,
                  Bradford Park Avenue, Tranmere Rovers.

Goalkeeper Arthur Norman Lewis was a safe handler of the ball, sound in his overall ability, courageous and totally committed. Educated in Wolverhampton, on leaving school he took employment as an assembler on the shop floor in a local car factory, playing in goal for the Sunbeam Works team at weekends.

Spotted by an eagle-eyed Wolves scout, he was asked to attend a trial match at Molineux and after impressing the watching gallery was taken on as a full-time professional in July 1928.

Standing 5ft 10in tall and weighing 12st, Norman conceded 57 goals in 30 first-team appearances in his initial season with the club. Impressed with his performances, Stoke manager Tom Mather moved in and persuaded his counterpart at Molineux, Jack Addenbrooke, to sell him to the Potters. An agreement was drawn up and in May 1929 Norman moved to the Victoria Ground for what was to prove a bargain fee of just £250.

He replaced Dick Williams between the posts seven games into the 1929–30 season and quickly became an automatic choice, retaining his position with some impressive displays while making 18 senior appearances. In 1930–31 he added 39 outings to his tally and the following season was outstanding, starring in 41 games as the Potters finished third in the Second Division. He stood between a defeat or a draw on many occasions and was quite brilliant in the home fixtures against Chesterfield (won 2–1), Nottingham Forest (2–1), Plymouth Argyle (3–2), his former club Wolves (3–2), Swansea Town (0–0) and Millwall (0–0), while he played out of his skin in the away fixtures at Charlton (1–1), Manchester United (1–1) and Bristol City (0–0). He received a standing ovation when he left the field at Ashton Gate, having saved a penalty. It is believed that Norman saved six penalties during his time with Wolves and the Potters.

The team was now fully equipped to challenge for promotion, but for the 1932–33 campaign manager Mather surprisingly installed the former Walsall and Welsh international Roy John as first-choice 'keeper, Norman dropping into the reserves.

John played in all but one game that season as the Potters won the Championship and thus returned to the top flight. Obviously disappointed, Norman battled on and although John kept his place, missing only the odd game here and there through injury and international duty, he was sold to Preston North End in June 1934, allowing Norman to regain his first-team place.

He starred in 37 matches in 1934–35 and 17 more the following season, taking his overall tally of senior appearances with the club to a creditable 170, keeping 44 clean sheets in the process.

Stoke made a modest profit when, in May 1936, they sold Norman to Bradford Park Avenue for £300, this after the former Huddersfield Town 'keeper Norman Wilkinson had established himself in goal. At that time Norman stood in second place behind Bob Dixon for having appeared in the most senior games as a goalkeeper for the Potters (170 to Dixon's tally of 200).

He remained with the Yorkshire club for six months, having just two outings, before transferring to Tranmere Rovers in November 1936 for £250. He went on to help the Birkenhead club win the Third Division North Championship and continued playing for them during the first part of the war, eventually retiring in May 1942 when he was almost 34 years of age.

His career realised well over 200 club appearances and after folding away his jersey he returned to Wolverhampton, where he lived the rest of his life, watching his football at Molineux and making only the occasional visit to the Victoria Ground. Norman was 64 when he died in 1972.

Bobby Liddle

Born: 11 April 1908, Gateshead
Died: 12 April 1972, Bilborough, Nottingham

Stoke City record:
Appearances: League 297, FA Cup 19, wartime 152
Goals: League 61, FA Cup 3, wartime 28
Debut: League, 25 August 1928 v Nottingham Forest (a) won 5-1

Also played for: Washington Colliery FC

Bobby Liddle was a star performer for Stoke City for over a decade and continued to shine during World War Two, when his appearances were restricted. Discovered in north-east England, he was working down a coal mine when he signed as a full-time professional for the Potters as a 19-year-old in January 1928.

A dashing, clever and extremely versatile footballer who played with great zest both at home and away, Bobby was a shade on the small side at only 5ft 7in tall and 10st 7lb, but he was a tough character who loved a challenge.

A forward who could play anywhere, he favoured the right-wing position over the left and started his Potters career there. With the emergence of a certain Stanley Matthews, who immediately slotted into the team at outside-right, followed by Joe Johnston, who took over from Bobby Archibald and bedded himself in on the left, Bobby remained in the team as an inside-forward and did superbly well, earning high praise from manager Tom Mather on many occasions. After moving south from his Gateshead home, he had to wait until August 1928 before making his League debut. Taking over from Jack Cull on the right wing against Nottingham Forest at the City Ground, he celebrated with a smartly taken goal and had a hand in two others in an emphatic 5–1 victory.

He made 11 more senior appearances that season (all but one at outside-right) and appeared in 25 matches the next term, when he was switched to inside-left. He scored six times, including a brace in an exciting 3–3 draw at Notts County. In 1930–31 Bobby missed only one League game (at home to Nottingham Forest through illness) and netted 15 goals, which would prove to be his best return for the club. He started off in the inside-left berth but was then switched to the right wing after first Joe Mawson and

then Tommy Sale came forward to claim their places alongside Archibald.

An adaptable player with an eye for goal, Bobby continued to produce the goods and was once again in fine form in 1931–32, scoring 11 times in 44 senior outings as the Potters edged up to third in the Second Division table. The very next season, he formed part of a tremendous front line which scored 78 goals as Stoke City clinched the Championship and so regained their place in the top flight, relinquished some 10 years earlier in 1923.

The Potters' forward line at this juncture comprised Bobby Liddle (seven goals), Harry Ware (seven), Joe Mawson (16) or Jack Palethorpe (eight), Tommy Sale (11) and Joe Johnson (15). Matthews had been injured and played in only 15 games (one goal).

Establishing themselves back with the big boys, Stoke had a decent enough 1933–34 season, Bobby netting six times in his 36 starts. He struck 10 goals in 39 appearances in 1934–35 and followed up with five in 38 in 1935–36, but during the three seasons leading up to World War Two he registered just two in 43 outings.

During the war he added a further 152 first-team appearances to his overall tally and scored another 28 goals, finishing with a combined League, FA Cup and wartime record of 92 goals in 468 appearances.

Bobby was 36 years of age when he announced his retirement as a player in May 1944. At that point he was appointed as the club's senior trainer, a position he held until the summer of 1953, when he quit football altogether having given Stoke City Football Club 25 years' unbroken service.

In later years he bought a house near Nottingham and was 64 when he died in 1972, having enjoyed watching the Potters win the League Cup against Chelsea.

John McCue

Born:	22 August 1922, Longton, Stoke-on-Trent
Died:	19 November 1999, Longton, Stoke-on-Trent

Stoke City record:

Appearances:	League 502, FA Cup 40, wartime 133
Goals:	League 2
Debut:	Wartime, 13 May 1940 v Tranmere Rovers (a) lost 5–1
	FA Cup, 5 January 1946 v Burnley (h) won 3–1
Also played for:	Oldham Athletic, Macclesfield Town

Archetypal full-back John McCue had a wonderful career with Stoke City. Well-proportioned and strong in the tackle, he always gave 100 per cent out on the field of play, never shirked a tackle and was a fighter to the last.

Educated at Longton Council School, he joined the Potters two days after his 15th birthday in 1937 and signed full-time professional forms in April 1940. Soon afterwards he made his first appearance for the seniors in a friendly against Nottingham Forest and then starred in his initial competitive game at Tranmere in a Regional Wartime League fixture, partnering Harry Brigham in a 5–1 defeat.

John went on to appear in 133 games for the club during the hostilities, but when League football resumed in August 1946 he had to sit out the opening four matches due to a niggling injury before slipping into the left-back position. He retained his position virtually unchallenged for the next 13 years, although towards the end of his service with Stoke he did switch to the right flank, allowing Tony Allen to don the number-three shirt.

He was twice an ever present, in 1951–52 and 1958–59, missed only one game in 1954–55 and was absent three times in each of the 1948–49, 1950–51 and 1956–57 seasons. In fact, he made 33 or more League appearances for the Potters on 12 occasions and his best unbroken spell in the first team was a run of 77 consecutive League and Cup games from 2 November 1957 to 22 August 1959 inclusive.

John had 22 full-back partners during his time with the Potters, with Billy Mould, George Bourne and Tony Allen proving to be his longest-serving companions.

A very sporting player, hardly ever spoken to by the referee and certainly never sent off, John was a dedicated professional who loved his football. He was much admired by the supporters and acted as a father figure to several of the younger players who were at the club with him.

With his sweet and precise left foot, he became the first player to appear in 500 League games for the Potters, reaching that milestone in March 1960 when Charlton Athletic spoilt his party with a 3–1 win at the Victoria Ground. Earlier in the season, John had broken Bob McGrory's club record of 479 League appearances.

In total John made 675 appearances at competitive level for the club – only Eric Skeels has played in more matches – and surprisingly he scored just two goals. Both came in League games: the first was in a 3–2 home win over Middlesbrough in May 1952 while his second earned the team a point from a 1–1 draw with Bristol Rovers at Eastville in December 1954. Unfortunately, for all his qualities and outstanding displays, John's only representative honour in the game was to appear in four 'Test Matches' for the FA on their tour to Australia in 1950–51.

With Tony Allen and Tom Ward occupying the two full-back positions (and Ron Wilson in reserve), John left the Victoria Ground in September 1960 to sign for Oldham Athletic on a free transfer. He made 56 appearances for the Latics before going on to assist non-League side Macclesfield Town, announcing his retirement at the age of 40 in May 1963.

In 1961–62 John was granted a belated testimonial match when the full Stoke City team played his selected XI at the Victoria Ground. A crowd of 5,000 witnessed a 6–2 victory for Stoke, but John benefited well from the evening's entertainment.

A qualified physical education instructor, John continued to attend Stoke City home games and was always a welcome visitor to the Victoria Ground. He was 77 when he died in 1999.

Bob McGrory

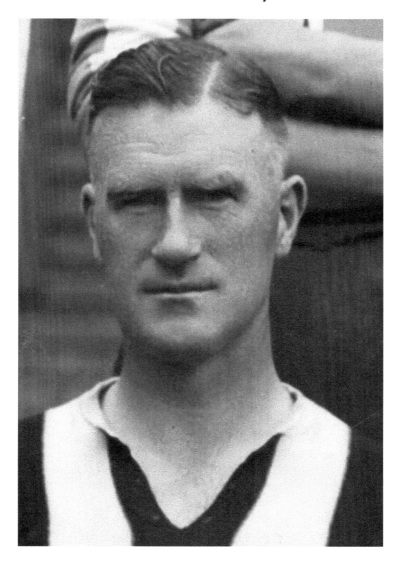

Born: 17 October 1891, Bishopton, Renfrewshire
Died: 23 May 1954, Glasgow

Stoke City record:
Appearances: League 479, FA Cup 32
Debut: League, 2 May 1921 v Barnsley (h) won 3–2

Also played for: Milgarvie FC (Scotland), Dumbarton, Burnley
Managed: Stoke City, Merthyr Tydfil

Bob McGrory was a dour, fearless full-back who earned a reputation for his strong, no-nonsense tackling and powerful kicking with the Scottish club Dumbarton before joining Burnley for £3,000 in August 1914. He spent just the one season at Turf Moor, making only three League appearances, and in April 1921 Stoke boss Arthur Shallcross moved in and secured his services as player-coach.

Bob would remain at the Victoria Ground for the next 31 years, until May 1952, serving the Potters as a defender in 511 League and FA Cup games – only Eric Skeels and John McCue have appeared in more senior matches for the club. He had one unbroken run of 101 games between March 1926 and September 1929, skippering the team on many occasions. In the summer of 1932 he was appointed team manager of the reserves, and he also served as assistant manager before finally taking over as team boss on a full-time contract in June 1935. He remained in office for 17 years, announcing his resignation at the end of the 1951–52 season at the age of 60.

He played his last competitive game for the Potters on 4 May 1935, starring in a 2–0 win at home to Huddersfield Town in front of 10,000 fans. Bob was an ever present in his final season, the third time he had appeared in every first-team match in one campaign.

A regular in the side from day one until the end of 1932, only injury kept him out of the action. He was hardly ever spoken to by a referee, and certainly never cautioned or suspended.

Slipping gracefully into the reserves having already made 430 appearances for the senior side, he played in eight League games during the 1932–33 season (deputising for Billy Spencer). Bob was recalled on a permanent basis the following season at the age of 42, and kept on playing at the highest level until he kicked his last ball in earnest just a few months short of his 44th birthday. Bob is now on record as being the second-oldest player ever to wear a Stoke City shirt, behind the great Stanley Matthews. He helped the Potters win the Third Division North Championship in 1926–27 and the Second Division title in 1932–33.

When Tom Mather surprisingly left the Victoria Ground to take charge of Newcastle United, Bob took to management like a duck to water. He made very few changes to personnel within the club and gradually replaced ageing players with some very talented youngsters as he slowly built up a strong and resourceful side.

One of his best buys was probably centre-forward Tommy Sale, and before World War Two he also recruited Billy Mould, Harry Oscroft and Jock Kirton (one of his first signings). Bob persuaded Frank Bowyer, future England international Neil Franklin, John McCue, Frank Mountford and Johnny Sellars all to turn professional. After the hostilities he secured the services of Tom Johnston and Irishman Sammy Smyth among others.

Bob eventually stepped down as boss, handing over his duties to Frank Taylor having managed the team in 192 League games and won 90 of them. He guided the Potters to within two points of the First Division title in 1947, finishing third after losing the last game of the season to Sheffield United when victory at Bramall Lane would have put them above champions Liverpool.

Bob had a brief spell in charge of Welsh non-League side Merthyr Tydfil before quitting football altogether early in 1953. He remained in close contact with Stoke City until his death a year later.

Bob's exact year of birth has been given as 1891, 1894 and 1895 in various reference books but with guidance from other statisticians I have gone for 1891.

Sammy McIlroy

Born: 2 August 1954, Belfast

Stoke City record:
Appearances: League 132+1, FA Cup 6, League Cup 5
Goals: League 14
Debut: League, 10 February 1982 v Sunderland (a) won 2–0

Also played for: Manchester United, Manchester City, IS Orgryte (Sweden), Bury, FC Modling (Norway), Preston North End, Northwich Victoria (player-manager), Northern Ireland (88 full caps)
Managed: Ashton United, Macclesfield Town, Stockport County, Morecambe, Northern Ireland

Samuel 'Sammy' Baxter McIlroy was educated at Ashfield School and joined Manchester United as an apprentice in August 1969, turning professional two years later.

He was, in fact, the last youth player signed by Matt Busby, therefore making him the last of the Busby Babes. He was 17 years of age when he scored on his League debut in a 3–3 draw in the derby against Manchester City at Maine Road in November 1971 but was not able to win a regular first-team place until 1974–75, by which time United were not in the top flight, having been relegated at the end of the previous campaign.

Sammy played in every game that season, scored seven League goals, three of them proving vital, and duly collected a Second Division Championship medal for his efforts. The following season he was bitterly disappointed when Southampton won the FA Cup Final, beating United 1–0. He quickly perked up and played his part a year later when United lifted the trophy at Liverpool's expense, only to collect a second runners'-up medal in 1979 when Arsenal won the trophy 3–2.

Initially a forward, Sammy was successfully switched into midfield in the late 1970s and did an excellent job in the engine room for both club and his country, Northern Ireland.

At international level, he won 88 full caps and scored five goals. He played in all of the country's matches during the 1982 World Cup Finals, when Northern Ireland defeated the host nation Spain and advanced to the second round. Four years later he captained the team and played every match in the 1986 World Cup Finals in Mexico.

After scoring 70 goals in 418 senior appearances for United, Sammy was transferred to Stoke City in February 1982 for £350,000. He spent three and a half years at the Victoria Ground and gave the 'Stokies' plenty to cheer about with his never-say-die attitude and total commitment.

He made 18 League appearances during the second half of the 1981–82 season and missed only one game in 1982–83 and two the following season.

In 1984–85 he struggled with an injury for a few weeks but still managed 34 outings in the First Division. Unfortunately, his efforts were all in vain as the Potters finished bottom of the pile with only 17 points and were duly relegated to the Second Division.

In August 1985, Sammy left Stoke and returned to Manchester, joining United's arch rivals City. After a loan spell in Sweden with IS Orgryte, he assisted Bury (from March 1987) and then played for the Norwegian club FC Modling from January to August 1988 before becoming player-coach (under manager John McGrath) of Preston North End, a position he held for 18 months. He retired as a player in 1990 with 800 appearances and 104 goals under his belt.

In July 1991, Sammy took his first managerial appointment with Northwich Victoria. He held office until October 1992 and two months later took charge of Ashton Town, switching his allegiance to Macclesfield Town in May 1993. He guided the 'Silkmen' into the Football League in 1997 (after they had been refused entry two years earlier because of ground regulations) and remained boss at Moss Rose until January 2000, when he left to take charge of the Northern Ireland national team, holding office for three years.

Unfortunately he didn't have much luck with the Irish, who won only five of 29 matches, all in Sammy's first year. The side failed to score a single goal in 13 qualifying matches for Euro 2004. Upon completion of the qualifying matches, Sammy resigned to re-enter club management, replacing Carlton Palmer at Stockport County, whom he managed until November 2004.

A year later, he took over as caretaker manager of Conference side Morecambe (November 2005) and made the move a permanent one soon afterwards (May 2006) when he replaced his close friend Jim Harvey. Sammy had a terrific first season in charge, leading Morecambe into the Football League with a 2–1 Conference Pflay-off Final victory over Exeter City at the new Wembley in front of more than 40,000 fans.

John Mahoney

Born: 29 September 1946, Cardiff

Stoke City record:
Appearances: League 270+12, FA Cup 14+1, League Cup 22+2, others 8
Goals: League 25, FA Cup 1, League Cup 1, others 1
Debut: League, 18 March 1967 v Sunderland (h) won 3–0

Also played for: Ashton United, Crewe Alexandra, Middlesbrough, Swansea
                 City, Wales (3 Under-23 and 51 full caps)
Managed: Bangor City (two spells), Newport County, Carmarthen Town

John Mahoney's playing career spanned almost 19 years, from August 1964 to March 1983. During that time he appeared in 652 matches, 489 of them in the Football League.

Born into a sporting family (his father Joe played both rugby union and rugby league), John did well with Ashton United (from 1964) before joining Crewe Alexandra in March 1966. He spent 12 months at Gresty Road, during which time he was capped by Wales against Northern Ireland at Under-23 level. In March 1967 he moved to Stoke City for £160,000, signed by Tony Waddington, who needed flair and mobility in midfield.

John made his debut against Sunderland, lining up alongside George Eastham and Dennis Viollet. He did well, had a hand in one of the goals in a 3–0 win and came close to scoring himself on two occasions. He was later joined in midfield by fellow countryman Roy Vernon and ended the season with eight appearances and three goals to his name.

The following season John made 32 appearances when he was accompanied in midfield by Calvin Palmer, among others. He was also recognised by his country at senior level for the first time, manager Dave Bowen selecting him for the 3–0 defeat against England in October 1967. This was the first of 51 full caps he would win, and he also added two more Under-23 caps to his tally in 1970 and 1971.

In fact, John – or Josh, as he was called – played with passion and commitment for his country for a decade, and these qualities were abundantly displayed in the crucial European Championship qualifying match against Austria in November 1975 when he helped Wales reach the final stages of this competition for the very first time.

Prior to that, in 1968–69 John was joined in midfield by Mike Bernard, and their presence and determination helped the team finish 19th, avoiding relegation by three points. Over the next three seasons – 1969–72 – John was superb as Stoke played some wonderful football. He kept things rolling in centre-midfield where he was joined by Terry Conroy, while Peter Dobing and Jimmy Greenhoff also pulled their weight.

In each of the latter two campaigns, the Potters were FA Cup semi-finalists, but lost both times in a replay to Arsenal, with the Gunners completing the League and Cup double in 1971.

In 1972 the Potters went to Wembley for the first time in their history, beating Chelsea 2–1 in the League Cup Final. John was outstanding against the London club, matching Alan Hudson and generally running the midfield, his surging runs causing all sorts of problems to the defenders.

After more than 10 years at the Victoria Ground, John moved to Middlesbrough for £90,000 in August 1977. He stayed at Ayresome Park until July 1979, when he switched to Swansea City in a £100,000 deal. After gaining a Welsh Cup-winners' medal in 1981, a broken leg suffered in a League game against Brighton & Hove Albion in March 1983 ended John's career. He worked in the commercial department at the Vetch Field for a short time before entering management with Bangor City in September 1984.

He had three successful years with the Welsh club before resigning when Bangor's financial problems began to mount. Taken on as assistant manager of Newport County, who had just been relegated from the Football League, John was thrust into the hot seat when boss Eddie May left on the eve of the 1988–89 season. He remained at the helm until County were wound up in April 1989.

John managed the Welsh semi-professional team for one match against England before returning for a second spell as boss of Bangor City in May 1991, later managing Carmarthen Town.

Johnny Malkin

Born: 9 November 1925, Normacot, Staffordshire
Died: 19 May 1994, Stoke-on-Trent

Stoke City record:
Appearances: League 175, FA Cup 15
Goals: League 23, FA Cup 4
Debut: League, 27 March 1948 v Everton (a) won 1–0

A pupil at Queensbury Road School in Stoke-on-Trent, Johnny Malkin served as a soldier in the British Army from 1941 and played for the British Army of the Rhine team. After a trial with the Potters in August 1946, he was taken on by the club as a part-time professional at the Victoria Ground the following month before signing as a full-time professional when he was demobbed in July 1947. He spent the next nine years with Stoke City Football Club, during which time he accumulated a total of 190 first-team matches and scored 27 goals.

A strong, diminutive winger with good pace and a powerful right-foot shot, Johnny was very positive. He loved taking on his full-back on the outside and became a huge favourite with the Victoria Ground crowd. He was certainly unlucky, in some respects, to have had Stanley Matthews occupying the number-seven position during his early years at the club, and even when Stan moved to Blackpool in 1947 Johnny still remained in the reserves behind George Mountford, who took over on the right wing and performed exceedingly well.

Johnny finally got the nod in 1949–50 when he was called upon to fill both flanks. There was an old wives' tale that the number-seven shirt at Stoke City was unlucky for the player who wore it after Stanley Matthews had relinquished it in 1947, but Johnny scotched that rumour by giving the Potters excellent service from the right wing as well as from the left.

Johnny didn't play much football (certainly at a competitive level) until he entered the army as a 15-year-old. He then turned out for his unit quite regularly and was actually playing for the BOAR team in a representative match when a scout from Stoke City spotted his undoubted talent. Potters manager Bob McGrory was duly informed and things began to materialise quite quickly. After starring in two trial matches, Johnny became a Potter, and he never looked back.

Johnny made his League debut in front of more than 44,000 spectators at Goodison Park on Easter Saturday 1948, playing his part in a fine 1–0 win, Frank Mountford's goal deciding the contest against a strong Everton side. He played in four more League games that season, versus Burnley, Chelsea, Aston Villa and Wolves, and he scored his first senior goal in a 3–0 home win over Chelsea.

In season 1948–49 he was called into action just six times (in place of George Mountford) and in 1949–50 appeared on 29 occasions, 12 on the left wing before switching to the right to allow new signing Harry Oscroft to come into the team.

Annoyingly for Johnny, Alec Ormston and Oscroft became the favoured wingers in 1950–51 but he was back in the frame the following season when he played in 32 matches, netting his first FA Cup goal in a third-round replay win over Sunderland.

Johnny played in 26 more competitive games in 1952–53 and 42 the following season, which turned out to be his best total of senior appearances in any one campaign. He reached double figures for the first time in the goal stakes, netting 11 times – 10 in the League – including braces against Leicester City and Nottingham Forest in successive matches in September.

After making another 31 appearances for the first team in 1953–54 and 11 at the start of the next campaign, unfortunately Johnny suffered knee ligament damage during the away Second Division encounter at Leicester in October 1955. He never regained full fitness despite strenuous attempts and long periods in the treatment room.

On the advice of a leading orthopaedic surgeon, he was forced to retire in the summer of 1956 at the age of 30. Johnny was later rewarded with a testimonial with fellow teammate George Bourne and he received £855 plus an extra grant from the club.

He was 69 when he died in 1994.

Jackie Marsh

Born: 31 May 1948, Newcastle-under-Lyme

Stoke City record:
Appearances: League 346+9, FA Cup 32, League Cup 35, others 11
Goals: League 2
Debut: League, 19 August 1967 v Arsenal (a) lost 2–0

Also played for: Los Angeles Aztecs (NASL), Bulowa (Hong Kong), Northwich Victoria

Jackie Marsh followed a number of other locally born players of his generation to the Victoria Ground and, like Alan Bloor, Mike Pejic and Denis Smith, he went on to the ultimate accolade of gaining a League Cup-winners' medal at Wembley in 1972.

An exceptionally fine full-back, confident in possession with a good turn of pace, he was also a superb crosser of the ball, regularly sending it flat and also deep into the opposing penalty area for the likes of John Ritchie, Jimmy Greenhoff and Ian Moores, and later for John Tudor, Viv Busby and Brendan O'Callaghan.

Jackie certainly played an important role in the Potters' success in the early 1970s and was one of the first names on manager Tony Waddington's team sheet, forming a fine full-back partnership initially with Alex Elder, then Pejic and later with Alec Lindsay and Geoff Scott. He joined the Potters as a 15-year-old apprentice in 1963 and turned professional in June 1965. Making his senior debut against Arsenal at Highbury in August 1967 when he deputised for the injured Eric Skeels in a 2–0 defeat, Jackie was kept completely in the dark by his boss Waddington right up until the very last minute, and not even the announcer on the tannoy system knew who the Stoke City right-back was going to be!

He did quite well against the Gunners, marking tricky winger George Armstrong, but had to wait until the following season before gaining a regular place in the first team, taking over the number-two shirt from Skeels, who was moved forward into the right-half position.

Jackie made 35 appearances in 1968–69 and scored his first senior goal in a 3–1 defeat at Manchester City in late March. As the years and games rolled by, only one more goal came Jackie's way for the club – a fine low drive in a 2–0 home League win over Burnley in October 1974.

In 1969–70 he missed six League games and the same number again in 1970–71, when he helped the Potters reach the semi-final of the FA Cup, which they lost in a replay to the subsequent double winners, Arsenal. He and his teammates suffered the same disappointment 12 months later when once again the Gunners won through to the FA Cup Final, again at the second attempt.

In 1972 Jackie did go to Wembley for the League Cup Final showdown with Chelsea and played as well as anyone on the pitch that afternoon as the Potters beat the Londoners 2–1 to lift the first major trophy in the club's long history.

Jackie played in 65 competitive matches in season 1971–72 and he continued to pile up appearances after that, starring in 44 games in 1972–73, 37 in 1973–74, 45 in 1974–75 and 31 in 1975–76. Injuries and suspensions curtailed his outings in 1976–77 and he managed only 20, his lowest tally since his debut campaign of 1967–68. After two more useful seasons, during which he amassed a further 64 appearances his final total with the club stood at a healthy 433. Jackie tried his luck in the North American Soccer League with Los Angeles Aztecs as a loan player during the second half of the campaign but was released by the club in May 1979.

At that point he chose to sign a short-term contract with the strong Hong Kong club Bulowa before returning to England to play for Northwich Victoria. He spent four seasons in non-League football, from August 1980 to May 1984, before retiring at the age of 36.

After hanging up his boots Jackie took employment as a sales representative in Stoke-on-Trent, attending Potters home matches at the Victoria Ground on the odd occasion.

Sir Stanley Matthews, CBE

Born: Stoke-on-Trent, 1 February 1915
Died: Hanley, Stoke-on-Trent, 5 May 1999

Stoke City record:
Appearances: League 318, FA Cup 37, wartime 69
Goals: League 54, FA Cup 8, wartime 8
Debut: League, 19 March 1932 v Bury (a) won 1–0

Also played for: Blackpool, (wartime guest for Airdrieonians, Arsenal, Crewe
                Alexandra, Manchester United, Morton, Rangers and
                Wrexham), Toronto City (Canada), England (29 wartime and 54
                full caps).
Managed: Port Vale, Hibernians (Malta)

Stanley Matthews, 'the Wizard of Dribble', was a superbly gifted right-winger and one of the greatest footballers to grace the world stage. Blessed with dazzling skills and wonderful ball control, he was able to beat most defenders for pace over 25–30 yards, could centre with pin-point accuracy and scored some splendid goals. He regularly bemused and bewildered the toughest of opponents and the tightest of defences.

Stan represented England schoolboys in 1929 and four years later won a Second Division Championship medal with the Potters, making his full international debut in 1934 against Wales and celebrating the occasion with a goal in a 4–0 victory. In 1937 he netted a hat-trick for his country in a 5–4 win over Czechoslovakia and when World War Two broke out he had already appeared in 17 matches for England. During the hostilities, as well as playing in several services games, 24 wartime and five Victory internationals, he won a League North Cup-winners' medal with Blackpool in 1943. Injuries, however, started to interrupt his performances and as a result he dropped out of favour at Stoke. Despite vigorous protests from the Potters supporters to keep him, he was sold to Blackpool in 1947.

With Stan in the team, the Seasiders reached two FA Cup Finals in four years and lost them both. In 1953 it was third-time lucky for Stan and his colleagues as they triumphed 4–3 over Bolton, courtesy of some brilliant wing play by Stan and a Mortensen hat-trick. Blackpool trailed 3–1 but, inspired by Stan, they fought back and Bill Perry struck the winning goal late on after some wonderful trickery by Stan.

Stan won his 54th and final cap in 1957, at the age of 42 years and 103 days, the oldest footballer ever to play for England. He scored 11 international goals. Surprisingly, he played in only one game in the 1950 World Cup Finals and two in the 1954 Finals, and he was left behind in 1958 to the dismay of the public.

In 1961 he returned to relegation-threatened Stoke and the crowds at the Victoria Ground increased fivefold, leaping up from 8,400 to 36,000. Within a year the Potters had escaped the drop and were Second Division champions.

Stan played his final League game on 6 February 1965 aged 50 years and five days, having served the Potters, in two spells, for 19 years. He played League football for 32 years and 324 days. The record books show that Matthews played in at least 2,000 football matches, 1,127 of them at a competitive level. Soon after leaving Stoke he received a Knighthood to add to the CBE awarded to him in 1957. He was voted Footballer of the Year in 1948 and 1963 and received the accolade of European Footballer of the Year in 1956. Stan appeared in almost 800 competitive matches at club level, 701 in the Football League (332 with Stoke, 369 with Blackpool). He scored 80 goals.

Born the son of Hanley's boxing barber Jack Matthews, he attended Wellington Road School and played for Stoke St Peter's before joining the Potters as an amateur in July 1930, turning professional in February 1932. He made his League debut for Stoke in March 1932 but it was two years before he established himself in the first team.

Prior to his return to Stoke in 1961, Stan assisted the Canadian club Toronto City (June–September 1961) and when he left the Victoria Ground, he became Port Vale's general manager, taking over as team manager in May 1967 and remaining in office until April 1968 when he was appointed youth coach. He went on to manage the Maltese club Hibernians and thereafter coached in South Africa (Soweto), Australia, the US and Canada before returning to the Potteries to become Stoke City's president, a position he held until his death in 1999. He was honorary vice-president of Blackpool and president of the City Vale Club.

Willie Maxwell

Born: 21 September 1876, Arbroath
Died: 7 December 1940, Scotland

Stoke City record:
Appearances: League 156, FA Cup 17
Goals: League 75, FA Cup 10
Debut: League, 2 September 1895 v Bolton Wanderers (h) won 2–0

Also played for: Hearts Strollers, Arbroath, Angus, Dundee, Heart of Midlothian, Third Lanark, Sunderland, Millwall Athletic, Bristol City, Scotland (1 full cap)

A tall, strong-running, dashing type of player with good speed and a powerful right-foot shot, Willie Maxwell was able to play in the centre-forward or inside-left positions and was excellent in both. He had a gift for scoring goals and during his lengthy career amassed an exceptionally fine record as a marksman.

Willie started out in junior football with Hearts Strollers before joining Arbroath as an amateur in August 1893. He became a solicitor's clerk in Dundee and, having the freedom of movement of a non-professional, he was able to assist several clubs, among them Angus (at county level), Dundee and Heart of Midlothian, assisting the latter in their Championship-winning season of 1894–95.

He joined the professional ranks when he decided to come to England to sign for Stoke as an 18-year-old in August 1895. He would remain a 'Potter' for exactly six years, and became a huge favourite with the supporters before returning to his homeland.

During his association with the club he averaged virtually a goal every other game, and collected his only full cap for Scotland against England at Celtic Park in April 1898, setting up Jamie Miller for his country's only goal in a 3–1 defeat. Only the second Stoke player (after Tom Hyslop) ever to represent Scotland, Willie is also the last.

Virtually a regular in the Potters' front line for the whole of his stay at the Victoria Ground, Willie had a relatively quiet first season, scoring just 11 goals in 27 games, including one on his debut in an opening day 2–0 home win over Bolton Wanderers. He also netted his first hat-trick for the club in a 5–0 FA Cup victory over Tottenham Hotspur.

In 1896–97, when he was partnered up front by the former Everton and Darwen forward Alan Maxwell (no relation), Willie netted 16 times, seven of his goals coming in five matches either side of Christmas. The following season he notched 12 goals before having his best scoring campaign with the club in 1898–99, when he weighed in with 19 (in 37 games).

His last two seasons produced a total of 27 goals (11 and 16 respectively), allowing him to finish with an excellent set of statistics: 85 goals in 173 appearances.

When he left the Victoria Ground (in August 1901) Willie returned to Scotland to sign for Third Lanark for £250. He spent just one season with the now defunct League club before re-entering the Football League with Sunderland in August 1902. After making just seven appearances for the Wearsiders (three goals scored) he switched to London and joined Millwall Athletic in the old Southern League. He did exceedingly well with the Lions, scoring 57 goals in 88 outings in two seasons, 34 coming in 1903–04 when he gained a London League Championship medal.

Willie's next port of call was Bristol City, who signed him for £200 in May 1905, and he again made a terrific impact at Ashton Gate. As an ever present he top scored with 25 League goals in his first season, helping City win the Second Division Championship. Willie continued to hit the target and in 1906–07 he struck home another 17 goals as City claimed the runners'-up spot in the top flight, the south-west club's highest-ever League finish.

After scoring 17 more goals in two more campaigns with City, the second of which saw him struggle desperately with injuries, 33-year-old Willie announced his retirement in May 1909, at which point he accepted an offer to coach the Belgian club FC Leopold of Brussels, later taking over as coach of that country's national side.

Willie scored a total of 222 senior goals in 418 appearances in Scottish and English football – a wonderful record.

Alex Milne

Born:	29 September 1889, Hebburn on Tyne
Died:	13 April 1970, Doncaster

Stoke City record:

Appearances:	Southern League 65, Football League 192, FA Cup 19, wartime 11
Debut:	Southern League, 25 December 1912 v West Ham United (a) lost 5–0
Also played for:	Hebburn Old Boys, West Stanley, Hebburn Argyle, Doncaster Rovers

Alex Milne, 5ft 10in tall and 12st in weight, was a solid performer in every sense of the word. A resilient defender, strong in the tackle, purposeful with his kicking and positive in the air, he regularly helped his goalkeeper out by clearing the ball from set pieces with one almighty leap and timely header. Indeed, he once sent the ball soaring 50 yards downfield with one of his mighty headed clearances.

Stoke boss Alfred Barker, who was steadily rebuilding his side in an effort to regain Football League status after some indifferent seasons in the old Southern League, recruited 23 year-old Alex from non-League football in north-east England in October 1912, paying just £50 for his services.

He went straight into the second team to enable him to get to know and learn the style of play the Potters were used to. After two months and some excellent displays he was eventually handed his senior debut on Christmas Day in the away Southern League game against a strong West Ham United side, slipping into the left-half position in place of Ernie Hodgkin, who was moved into the centre of defence in place of the injured Joey Jones.

Unfortunately, Alex, who was marking Danny Shea, didn't have the happiest of baptisms as the Potters crashed to an embarrassing 5–0 defeat, their heaviest in terms of goal-difference since March 1911. However, 24 hours later in the return fixture at the Victoria Ground, the contest was much closer, Stoke losing 1–0. This time Alex played well and retained his place for the next game, a 4–1 home win over Brighton and Hove Albion.

Alex made a total of 16 appearances in the first XI in 1912–13, and after establishing himself in the left-back position he followed up with 28 outings in each of the next two campaigns, gaining a Southern League Championship medal in the latter before World War One interrupted his and Stoke's progress.

During the hostilities Alex returned home to Hebburn to work in a munitions factory. He appeared in certain regional games for the Potters when he could, although it was quite a trek down from the North East to the Victoria Ground.

When competitive soccer resumed in August 1919, with Stoke reinstated in the Second Division of the Football League, Alex was switched over again to the right-back position, and from there he continued to produce some outstanding performances as part of a resolute Potters defence.

He was in superb form over the next four years, during which time he was ever present in 1920–21 in the left-back berth, missed only one match the following season when paired with the great Bob McGrory for the first time, and absent on six occasions in 1922–23.

A serious leg injury caused him to miss the whole of the 1923–24 campaign, his place going to Tom Howe, but he came back strongly in 1924–25 and made 19 appearances before having a very solid last season with the club, which took his overall appearance tally to a very creditable 287 (192 in the Football League).

Surprisingly, Alex never scored a goal for Stoke at any level, although he came close on a couple of occasions, striking the woodwork in home League games against Grimsby Town in November 1919 and Sheffield Wednesday in December 1921. Unfortunately he did find the net for his opponents, conceding own-goals against Newport County in December 1913 and Rochdale in April 1918.

On leaving the Victoria Ground in May 1926 Alex joined Doncaster Rovers. He continued playing for the Belle Vue club until May 1930, when he retired at the age of 41, having added a further 80 senior appearances to his tally achieved with the Potters.

Billy Mould

Born: 6 October 1919, Great Chell, Staffordshire
Died: 27 September 1999, Stoke-on-Trent

Stoke City record:
Appearances: League 177, FA Cup 17, wartime 69
Debut: League, 19 March 1938 v Wolverhampton Wanderers (a) drew
               2–2

Also played for: Summerbank FC, Crewe Alexandra

After playing magnificently at the heart of the defence in a local Sentinal Shield game for Stoke City's nursery team Summerbank FC, Billy Mould was signed by the Potters as an amateur in July 1936, along with Alec Ormston, and upgraded to professional status four months later, Ormston following him onto the senior payroll early in 1937.

After making good progress via the reserves, Billy made his Football League debut at centre-half in place of Arthur Turner in the away League game against Wolverhampton Wanderers in March 1938. Marking one of the best goalscorers in the game at that time, Dennis Westcott, 18-year-old Billy did exceptionally well. He shackled Westcott and helped his team earn a creditable point from a 2–2 draw in front of more than 32,000 spectators.

Billy retained his place in the half-back line for the remainder of that season, playing a blinder against Everton at home when he came face-to-face with another brilliant centre-forward in Tommy Lawton, and he made three appearances at the start of 1938–39 before Turner reclaimed his place after the Potters defence conceded nine goals.

After a spell in the second team, Billy returned to League action in mid-November, ironically against Wolves, and held his position until the end of February when injury let in Jack Bamber, Turner having been sold to Birmingham City. Billy came back into the side for two more games late on, then World War Two began.

He joined the Royal Artillery and was able to assist the Potters when his duties and commitments allowed. Indeed, during the hostilities he managed almost 70 outings for the club, having his best runs in the side in 1939–40 (29 games) and 1943–44 (20 outings) before suffering a serious wound to his right leg on active service in Normandy. As a result he spent quite some time in Ireland with a few of his colleagues, including Syd Peppitt and his best friend Alec Ormston.

Over a period of seven years from August 1939 to May 1946, Billy averaged 10 appearances per season, accumulating a total of 69 in various regional competitions for the Potters, helping them finish fifth in the Football League (North) section in 1941–42 and sixth the following season.

Back at the Victoria Ground for the start of the 1946–47 League campaign, Billy had by now lost his place in the first XI to a promising defender named Neil Franklin. He was switched to the right-back position where he replaced Harry Brigham, who was transferred to Nottingham Forest for £4,000.

Billy, who acted as captain on several occasions, produced some splendid displays at full-back while partnering John McCue and he remained in the number-two position, injuries apart, until January 1949, having missed only two League games in 1947–48.

Continuing to perform with authority, sound judgement and efficiency, Billy took his tally of League and Cup appearances with the Potters' up to a healthy-looking 194 (over 250 in all games) before leaving the Victoria Ground for Crewe Alexandra on a free transfer in July 1952. His place in the Potters line up went initially to the versatile Johnny Sellars before George Bourne came on the scene and later Brian Doyle.

At Gresty Road, Billy maintained his form over a period of two years, making a further 70 senior appearances for the Railwaymen and scoring his only goal in major football. He retired in July 1952 at the age of 34 to concentrate on running his own sports outfitters business in Stoke-on-Trent, which he had started some years earlier.

He continued to support the Potters and attended several games at the Victoria Ground until well into his 70s. In fact, the last time he saw a game was in 1993. Billy died in September 1999, just nine days short of his 80th birthday.

Frank Mountford

Born:	30 March 1923, Askern, Doncaster
Died:	27 June 2006, North Staffordshire

Stoke City record:

Appearances:	League 391, FA Cup 34, wartime 183
Goals:	League 21, FA Cup 3, wartime 54
Debut:	Wartime, 13 May 1940 v Tranmere Rovers (a) lost 5–1

Also played for: Campsall Boys, Derby County (guest)

The versatile Frank Mountford had a wonderful career with Stoke City. He moved to Stoke-on-Trent with his parents as a youngster and was still at school when he joined the Potters in July 1937. He then represented Campsall Boys, signing for Stoke as a professional aged 17 in April 1940.

After making just one senior appearance in the 1939–40 season, when he scored against Tranmere Rovers in a 5–1 defeat, he established himself in the first team during the next campaign while occupying the centre-forward position. He played splendidly and finished up as top scorer with 23 goals in 29 starts including two hat-tricks: the first in an opening day 4–3 home win over Notts County and the second in a 5–0 battering of Birmingham three months later. He also scored four times in a friendly victory over an RAF XI in mid-April.

Owing to injury and commitments to his country Frank appeared in only eight games in 1941–42, but he was back to full fitness and his best form in 1942–43 when he made 36 appearances in regional League and Cup games. He once again finished up as leading marksman with another 20 goals, which included another hat-trick in a 6–1 Cup quarter-final win over Crewe Alexandra.

In season 1943–44 Frank occupied four positions, starting off in the attack and finishing up in the centre of the defence, where he partnered England international Neil Franklin.

Continuing as centre-half (and at times as a wing-half) Frank held his form and his place with confidence, and in the last two wartime seasons he accumulated 88 more appearances, making his FA Cup debut in a third-round first-leg encounter against Burnley in January 1946. This, in fact, was the first of 425 senior appearances he made for the Potters, whom he served competently and professionally for 18 years.

Frank made the number-five shirt his own when Franklin decided to go and play his football in Bogota, and he was in outstanding form season after season, coming mightily close to gaining full international recognition – one feels if he had been with a top-line club then he would surely have played for England.

Always in the thick of the action, Frank possessed a strong but fair tackle. He was a powerful header of the ball and played in such a way that he regularly called upon the services of the club's trainer during the course of a game. Considered by opponents to be one of the fairest centre-halves in the game during the late 1940s and early 1950s, Frank rarely missed out on a 50–50 challenge and he always gave as good as he received.

Frank's former teammate and goalkeeper Dennis Herod said 'There were a number of great players during my time at the Victoria Ground, but one stood out for me. He was Frank Mountford, who served Stoke as player, trainer and coach and did everything well. I cannot speak too highly of him.'

Frank was 83 when he died in 2007.

Jackie Mudie

Born: 10 April 1930, Dundee
Died: 2 March 1992, Stoke-on-Trent

Stoke City record:
Appearances: League 88, FA Cup 1, League Cup 4
Goals: League 32, FA Cup 1
Debut: League, 4 March 1961 v Scunthorpe United (h) won 2–0

Also played for: Dunkeld Amateurs, Dundee Stodswell, Dundee, Lochee Harp,
                   Blackpool, Port Vale (player-manager), Scotland (17 full caps)
Also managed: Northwich Victoria

Jackie Mudie played for three local junior clubs and was also associated with Dundee before signing amateur forms for Blackpool from Lochee Harp in September 1946. He turned professional with the Seasiders in May 1947 but had to wait until March 1950 before making his League debut. He celebrated the occasion in style, scoring the only goal of the game at Liverpool in front of almost 34,000 spectators.

Jackie had a preference for leading the attack in spite of being slight and relatively small, standing barely 5ft 6in in his socks, but he mostly played as an inside-forward. A real livewire, he required constant vigilance from opposing defenders and was particularly dangerous inside the penalty area with his quick, neat manoeuvres.

In 1950–51 he finished second-highest scorer for Blackpool (behind Stan Mortensen) with 21 goals in 47 senior appearances. He played in that season's FA Cup Final defeat by Newcastle United, but after that disappointment Blackpool signed Ernie Taylor and, as a result, Jackie lost his place. He made only nine appearances in 1951–52 before eventually working himself back into the team. He netted a dramatic last-minute winner in the 1953 FA Cup semi-final victory over Tottenham Hotspur and soon afterwards helped Blackpool win the trophy by beating Bolton Wanderers 4–3 in a classic Wembley Final.

In August 1955, Jackie took over from the departed Mortensen as Blackpool's centre-forward and he proceeded to rattle in 22 goals in 43 games that season, following up with another 32 in 1956–57. His latter tally is still a record for a Blackpool player in the top flight of English football.

Jackie went on to score a total of 155 goals in 356 League and Cup appearances for the Bloomfield Road club, and while wearing the famous tangerine strip he also gained 17 full caps for Scotland, the first against Wales at Cardiff in 1956. He later notched a marvellous hat-trick in a 4–2 win over Spain at Hampden Park that secured his country's place in the 1958 World Cup Finals.

In March 1961, after spending almost 15 years with Blackpool, Jackie was signed by Stoke City manager Tony Waddington for just £7,000 and, just as he had done with the Seasiders, he scored on his debut for the Potters after just five minutes of a 2–0 home League win over Scunthorpe United.

The following season he was joined at the Victoria Ground by his former teammate at Bloomfield Road, Stanley Matthews, and together they helped transform the Potters from an adequate run-of-the-mill Second Division club into promotion material.

The Second Division Championship was won in 1962–63 as Jackie struck 20 goals (only three behind Dennis Viollet), but in effect it was to be his last season as a regular. He played only five more games during the opening months of the 1963–64 campaign before switching his allegiance to neighbouring Port Vale, signed in November 1963 for a healthy fee of £12,000 with defender Ron Wilson switching clubs as part of the deal. Jackie went on to become player-manager of the Valiants (from March 1965), subsequently working in tandem with general manager Stanley Matthews, who moved to Vale Park four months later.

Jackie maintained his association with football and among other things served as assistant manager and coach at Crewe Alexandra, managed non-League side Northwich Victoria, was trainer-coach briefly at Eastwood (Hanley) and acted as scout for the South African club Johannesburg Rangers. He attended games at the Victoria Ground (with his great pal and close friend Stanley Matthews) for many years. It came as a shock to a lot of people when he died in 1992, aged 61.

Jackie and Stanley Matthews were colleagues together at Blackpool, Stoke and Port Vale for a combined total of 18 years.

Brendan O'Callaghan

Born: 23 July 1955, Bradford

Stoke City record:

Appearances: League 255+10, FA Cup 10, League Cup 19
Goals: League 44, League Cup 3
Debut: League, 8 March 1978 v Hull City (h) won 1–0

Also played for: Doncaster Rovers, Oldham Athletic, Newcastle Town, Republic
of Ireland (7 full caps)

The versatile Brendan O'Callaghan was equally effective as a defender or an attacker. He netted 50 goals in nearly 300 first-class appearances for Stoke City in almost seven years with the club from March 1978 and February 1985.

A Yorkshireman, he joined Doncaster Rovers as an apprentice on leaving school in July 1971 and turned professional at Belle Vue two years later. He went on to score 77 goals in 212 games for Rovers over a period of four years before switching to the Victoria Ground for £40,000 a few weeks prior to the transfer deadline in 1978, being manager Alan Durban's first signing for the Potters.

'Just the man I need to boost our attack,' said Durban, and Brendan, who stood 6ft 2in tall, didn't let his boss down. He notched six goals in his first 15 outings at the end of that 1977–78 season, including the headed winner against Hull City on his debut in early March as a second-half substitute for Viv Busby. In fact, Brendan ran on to the field just as Stoke had been awarded a corner. He took up a position inside the penalty area and was in the right place to steer the ball home. He had been on the pitch for just eight seconds!

As leader of the attack the following season, Brendan, who continually unsettled defenders with his height, ended up as the team's top marksman with 16 goals, 15 coming in the League, and his valuable contribution went a long way in helping the Potters gain promotion to the First Division.

Strong in the air, he enjoyed getting on the end of corners and free-kicks floated in by Paul Maguire, and his flick-ons always seemed to cause trouble in opposing penalty areas. Certain match commentators and reporters believed that the Potters had this sort of set-piece working to a tee and that it was one of the best plans of attack in the country.

In May 1979 Brendan was called into the Republic of Ireland squad, making his international debut against West Germany in Dublin. This was the first of seven full caps he gained for his adopted country over a period of four years. His others were obtained against Argentina, Wales (twice), USA, Brazil (when Eire crashed 7–0) and Trinidad & Tobago.

In 1979–80, playing in the top flight for the first time in his career, Brendan found it much harder to find the net and managed only five League goals as the Potters successfully battled against relegation. During the early stages of the 1980–81 campaign, he was successfully switched from centre-forward to centre-half by manager Durban. He produced some outstanding displays and found time to score five goals, including a brave winner in the home League game against Crystal Palace.

With Alan Dodd playing alongside him at the heart of the Potters' defence, Brendan was once again in superb form during the first half of the 1981–82 season before being switched back into the attack by new manager Richie Barker.

'Big Bren' remained a dedicated Potter until February 1985, when he was sold to Oldham Athletic for a fee of £30,000. He helped the Latics avoid relegation but made only 10 senior appearances for the Boundary Park club before a serious groin injury (initially sustained at Wimbledon in April 1985) ended his senior career, which amounted to 110 goals in more than 450 competitive matches for clubs and country.

He later appeared in a handful of games for non-League side Newcastle Town (1990) while working in a local pottery factory. Soon afterwards Brendan returned to the Victoria Ground, where he became a well-respected and popular development officer in the Stoke City Community Department.

He was also on the PFA Management Committee, studied for a degree in business administration at the University of Dublin and appeared on a weekly sports programme for a radio station.

Jimmy O'Neill

Born: 13 October 1931, Dublin

Stoke City record:
Appearances: League 130, FA Cup 10, League Cup 9
Debut: League, 20 August 1960 v Plymouth Argyle (a) lost 3–1

Also played for: Bulfin United (Dublin), Everton, Darlington, Port Vale, Cork Celtic, Republic of Ireland (17 full caps)

Signed by Stoke City manager Tony Waddington from Everton for £5,000 in July 1960, Irish-born goalkeeper Jimmy O'Neill had been a full-time professional at Goodison Park for 11 years and appeared in 213 senior games for the Merseyside club before losing his place to Albert Dunlop.

Educated in Dublin, he played non-League football for Bulfin United before having a successful trial with Everton in 1948. Accepted as a full-time professional in May 1949, he was handed his Football League debut against Middlesbrough in August 1950 but didn't have the greatest of baptisms and conceded four goals in a heavy defeat at Ayresome Park. He made 10 appearances that season before becoming a regular between the posts from December 1951 until October 1956, helping the Merseysiders gain promotion from the Second Division in 1954 when he started in 28 matches.

Jimmy also represented the Republic of Ireland at full international level on 17 occasions during his time at Goodison Park, gaining his first cap against Spain in 1952 and his last against Czechoslovakia in 1959.

Blessed with a safe pair of hands, he was tall and strong and commanded his area with authority, competently dealing with high crosses while also being agile enough to get down to save ground shots. Reliable and dependable, he was also an expert at saving penalties, and during his time with Everton he prevented eight from being scored at reserve and first-team levels – and also stopped one 12-yard kick during his international career.

Taking over from Tommy Younger in the Potters' goal, Jimmy missed only two League games out of a possible 126 in his first three seasons at the Victoria Ground, helping Stoke City win the Second Division Championship in 1962–63 when he was an ever present, conceding only 50 goals (20 of them in home matches). He was quite brilliant at times and was certainly the man responsible for hard-earned victories over Huddersfield Town (2–1), Rotherham United (2–1), Plymouth Argyle (1–0 at Home Park), Cardiff City (1–0) and Chelsea (1–0 at Stamford Bridge). He also produced a string of saves when the Potters beat Sunderland 2–1 at the Victoria Ground as the promotion race was hotting up in mid-April.

Jimmy went on to appear in a total of 149 first-class games for the Potters (52 in succession) and kept a clean sheet in 48 of them – a terrific record of 32 per cent. He was replaced at the Victoria Ground by Lawrie Leslie in October 1963 and therefore missed out on Stoke's run to that season's League Cup Final. After a long spell in the Central League side he was transferred to Darlington for £1,500 in March 1964. He went on to make 30 appearances for the Quakers up to February 1965, when he chose to move back to the Potteries and sign for Stoke's arch rivals, Port Vale. He became a regular in the Valiants' team and played in 48 competitive games under manager Jackie Mudie, who had been a teammate of his in the Stoke side a few years earlier. He eventually lost his place through injury in March 1966.

After a two-month loan spell with the Irish club Cork Celtic (from December 1966 to January 1967) he returned to Vale Park as cover for Stuart Sharratt. Jimmy remained a Port Vale reserve until the end of the season, when he was given a free transfer. At that point Jimmy, then aged 35, announced his retirement from the game having played in well over 450 football matches for his four major clubs and his country. In later life he took employment as a taxi driver on Merseyside, making the occasional visit to watch a Stoke City home game.

Alec Ormston

Born:	10 February 1919, Hanley, Stoke-on-Trent
Died:	12 July 1975, Bentilee, Staffordshire

Stoke City record:

Appearances:	League 173, FA Cup 19, wartime 59
Goals:	League 29, FA Cup 1, wartime 19
Debut:	League, 20 November 1937 v Sunderland (h) drew 0–0

Also played for: Summerbank (Stoke), Hereford United, Stafford Rangers, Runcorn

A diminutive, enterprising left-winger with good pace, plenty of skill, aggression and tact, Alec Ormston, a former England schoolboy trialist, joined the Potters as an 18-year-old from local nursery club Summerbank in the summer of 1937 and immediately took on professional status.

He had to wait barely four months before making his senior debut in the inside-left position against the FA Cup holders Sunderland in a First Division League game at the Victoria Ground. He did extremely well and never looked out of his depth in a goalless draw in front of almost 32,000 spectators.

Alec made a further five appearances that season, all in the League and all as an inside-forward. With Frank Baker occupying the left-wing slot and playing pretty well, Alec couldn't get a look in and was called into action on only 10 occasions in 1938–39, nine of his outings coming at inside-left, at long last a chance came on the left flank, against Charlton Athletic at the Victoria Ground in April when Baker was a rare absentee.

During the wartime period Alec played when he could for the Potters, appearing in 59 regional League and Cup games and scoring 19 goals. His best season came in 1939–40, when he struck 11 goals in his 26 outings.

After the hostilities, he was first choice on the left wing for Stoke City's 1946–47 League campaign and played brilliantly at times, netting 21 goals in a total of 45 competitive appearances. He formed a fine partnership with his inside colleague Baker, while behind him he had the experienced Jock Kirton and full-back Johnny McCue.

The following season Alec scored five goals in 33 League and two FA Cup games, this time joined on the left side by cultured Irishman Jimmy McAlinden, who arrived at the club from Portsmouth.

Rewarded with three Football League representative call-ups (all against the League of Ireland), Alec was an ever present in the Potters' senior team in 1948–49 but managed to score only two goals – the first in a 4–2 home win over Derby County, his second in a 2–1 defeat by Aston Villa. However, Alec was now feeling some pressure from outside sources, with rumours flying around that the club was searching for a replacement left-winger.

He played in the opening three League games at the start of the 1949–50 season, missed the next 10, came back for two more and was then replaced on a permanent basis by Johnny Malkin before new signing Harry Oscroft took over on the left wing.

It was understood that manager Bob McGrory wanted to add some more sparkle to his attack and Alec, who was now fast approaching his 31st birthday, had lost some of his speed and indeed enthusiasm for the game.

After scoring almost 50 goals in more than 250 first-team matches, Alec reluctantly left the Victoria Ground to sign for Southern League side Hereford United in the summer of 1951. He later had a spell with Stafford Rangers and Runcorn, retiring in 1955 due to poor health. Indeed, he spent some time in Loggerheads Sanitorium on doctor's orders and after recovering full fitness he became licensee of a pub in Hanley. He later worked in the colliery offices and for a Madeley-based pottery company.

He also assisted the staff in the Stoke City promotions office based inside the Victoria Ground and was often seen chatting to supporters who had seen him wearing the red-and-white striped shirt in his heyday.

Alec, who attended his last Stoke City home game in 1972, died three years later at the age of 56.

Harry Oscroft

Born: 10 March 1926, Mansfield

Stoke City record:

Appearances: League 326, FA Cup 23
Goals: League 103, FA Cup 4
Debut: League, 14 January 1950 v West Bromwich Albion (a) drew
                 0–0

Also played for: Mansfield Colliery FC, Notts County (trial), Sheffield United
                    Trial), Mansfield Town, Port Vale, Brantham Athletic, Sutton
                    United

During World War Two, Harry Oscroft worked at a Mansfield colliery and served in the Royal Navy from the age of 17. In 1945 he got a job turning ladies' stockings in a Nottingham hosiery factory and every lunchtime he and his workmates used to go out and kick a tennis ball around on some wasteland. During one of these casual kick-arounds in mid-February 1947, the former England international and then Mansfield Town manager Roy Goodall passed by and a mate of Harry's called out 'Do you want an inside-forward?' Taken aback, Goodall stopped and surprisingly answered 'Yes I do'. He watched on and out of the blue asked Harry to come along for a trial at Field Mill. It was as simple as that.

Harry, who had earlier been a trialist in 1946 with both Notts County and Sheffield United and broke a bone in his left ankle with the latter, did well and was signed up immediately as an amateur, and after starring for the Stags' second team in a 10–0 victory over Frickley was handed his Football League debut against Queen's Park Rangers just a fortnight later. It was a fairy tale come true and within eight weeks he had become a full-time professional. He went on to score 41 goals in 113 outings over the next three and a bit seasons.

Harry netted a real beauty against Stoke City in an FA Cup tie in January 1948, and Potters boss Bob McGrory never forgot that goal. He was mightily impressed and kept an eye on the promising young Oscroft over the next few months. Indeed, he contacted Harry a couple of times asking him whether he would like to join the Potters. Nothing materialised but then, after former Stoke favourite Freddie Steele had taken charge at Field Mill, he convinced Harry that he should move to his former club and play at a higher level. After negotiations had been finalised, Harry (valued at around £22,000) moved to the Victoria Ground in January 1950 in a £30,000 deal which saw Verdi Godwin switch to Mansfield.

Just 24 hours after signing, Harry made his Potters debut in a 0–0 draw away to West Bromwich Albion, lining up on the left wing in place of Johnny Malkin, who switched to the right.

With the previous outside-left Alec Ormston slowly winding down his career, Harry retained the outside-left position virtually unchallenged over the next nine years, amassing a splendid record for the Potters of a goal every three senior games – the best scoring record by a winger in the club's history. In fact, Harry finished up with double figures in terms of goals six seasons running (1951–52 to 1956–57), topping the scoring charts twice in that period.

Unfortunately, the bulk of Harry's career with Stoke City was spent in the Second Division, and one feels that if he had been playing in the top flight he would surely have been considered for England honours. At the age of 33 he found himself out of the first team at the Victoria Ground and, along with reserve defender Peter Ford, he was transferred to neighbours Port Vale in exchange for Dickie Cunliffe, who was also a fast-raiding left-winger.

Harry spent two seasons with the Valiants, netting 12 times in 47 appearances while at the same time passing the milestone of 150 League goals in his career. He announced his retirement from first-class football in May 1961, moving to the Essex/Suffolk border to become player-manager of non-League side Brantham Athletic while also working for a local plastics manufacturing company.

Harry guided Brantham to victory in the Final of the Suffolk Senior Cup in 1962 and in later years assisted Sutton United as well as starring in local charity matches before finally hanging up his boots in 1988, aged 62.

Now residing in the village of Manningtree between Colchester and Ipswich, Harry is one of the oldest former Stoke City players alive today.

Calvin Palmer

Born: 21 October 1940, Skegness

Stoke City record:
Appearances: League 165, FA Cup 12, League Cup 12
Goals: League 24, League Cup 3
Debut: League, 18 September 1963 v Sheffield United (h) lost 2-0

Also played for: Skegness Town, Nottingham Forest, Sunderland, Cape Town (South Africa), Crewe Alexandra

Before he moved to Stoke City for a fee of £35,000 in September 1963, Calvin Palmer had made 106 senior appearances for Nottingham Forest, whom he joined from his home-town club, Skegness, as a full-time professional in March 1958. He made his League debut the following season but was not in Forest's FA Cup-winning team versus Luton Town.

Able to play as a full-back, central-defender or attacking wing-half, and even as an inside-forward, he made his League debut for the Potters 48 hours after signing. However, it was not a happy occasion as an inspired Sheffield United side spoiled the party by winning 2–0 at the Victoria Ground.

Calvin came in for the experienced Eddie Clamp at right-half against the Blades and competently held his place in the team, even when Clamp returned. In fact, he went on to play in 40 competitive games that season while wearing five different shirts (two, four, six, eight and 10) and scoring five goals, all in the League. His first strike came in a 3–2 win over Staffordshire rivals West Bromwich Albion at The Hawthorns. He also helped the Potters reach that season's League Cup Final, but for all his efforts Chelsea defeated Stoke City 4–3 on aggregate over two tightly contested legs.

In season 1964–65 Calvin, a big favourite of the Boothen End supporters, played in 36 out of the scheduled 42 League matches and in six of Stoke's eight major Cup fixtures, and once again he donned yet another shirt. This time it was number seven, which he wore for nine games halfway through the campaign when he linked up in midfield with Irish international Jimmy McIlroy, allowing the former Manchester United defender Maurice Setters to take over the right-half position. An unfairly publicised training ground dispute with Setters cost Calvin his place on Stoke's post season tour to the United States.

Switched to right-back by manager Tony Waddington virtually at the start of the 1965–66 season, Calvin played some of the best football of his career in this position. Initially he lined up alongside Eric Skeels and behind Dennis Viollet, and later had Tony Allen as his full-back colleague with Skeels in front of him.

Calvin netted twice in his 44 League and Cup outings that term, one of his goals earning a point in a 2–2 draw away against Championship-chasing Leeds United.

He added another 40 senior appearances to his tally in 1966–67, including one game at centre-forward, doing well in a 2–2 home draw with Arsenal on April Fool's day. Calvin was then made into a utility footballer during the first two-thirds of the 1967–68 campaign when manager Waddington used him as a full-back, wing-half, inside-forward and centre-forward. In fact, he wore the number-nine shirt eight times. He also scored a total of six goals, including a beauty in a 4–3 away win at Wolves and the winner at Southampton, both in the League.

Perhaps disillusioned in respect of not knowing where he was going to play from one week to the next, Calvin chose to leave the Potters in February 1968, joining Sunderland for a fee of £70,000. He did reasonably well at Roker Park, but a series of niggling injury problems, mainly to his knees, resulted in him making only 43 first-team appearances in two and a half seasons with the Wearsiders. He also netted five goals, his first against his former club Nottingham Forest a month after moving from the Victoria Ground. His other four strikes came in 1968–69, one of them in a 4–1 home victory over Stoke City in early March when future Potter Dennis Tueart also figured on the scoresheet.

In May 1970 he decided to quit the English scene and have a spell in South Africa with Cape Town, whom he served for 15 months. He returned to Football League action with lowly Crewe Alexandra in October 1971 but spent just four months at Gresty Road before quitting top-class football altogether in January 1972, mainly due to an ongoing knee injury.

Calvin, who accumulated well over 450 club appearances (350 at senior level) during his near 16-year career, now lives in his native Skegness.

Micky Pejic

Born: 25 January 1950, Chesterton, Staffordshire

Stoke City record:
Appearances: League 274, FA Cup 22, League Cup 29, others 11
Goals: League 6, League Cup 2
Debut: League, 8 April 1969 v West Ham United (a) drew 0–0

Also played for: Everton, Aston Villa, England (8 Under-23 and 4 full caps)
Managed: Leek Town, Northwich Victoria, Chester City

The son of a Serbian immigrant miner, Mike Pejic's professional playing career spanned 12 years, during which time he amassed well over 400 appearances at club level.

He started out as an apprentice with Stoke City in June 1967 after playing at weekends for the Corona Drinks team. He turned professional at the Victoria Ground in January 1968 and went on to play at a competitive level for Everton, Aston Villa and England (winning eight Under-23 and four full caps) until injury forced him into early retirement in May 1980 when he was only 30 years of age.

He made his League debut towards the end of the 1968–69 season before gaining a regular place in the side the following year, replacing Irish international Alex Elder at left-back as partner to Jackie Marsh.

Mike made 36 League appearances in 1969–70 and was an ever present the following season when the Potters reached the FA Cup semi-final, only to be beaten in a replay by Arsenal. That disappointment was quickly forgotten as Stoke reached and subsequently won the 1972 League Cup, beating Chelsea 2–1 in the Final at Wembley. Unfortunately, the very next month the Gunners again beat the Potters in the semi-final of the FA Cup to end Stoke's charge towards a second Wembley visit.

Mike won the first of his four full England caps against Portugal in Lisbon in April 1974, taking over

from Liverpool's Emlyn Hughes. He then appeared in the following three Home internationals as David Nish's partner but was allegedly dropped by new caretaker manager Joe Mercer in favour of Alec Lindsay because he 'didn't smile enough'.

After making 336 senior appearances for Stoke City, Mike was transferred to Everton for £135,000 in February 1977, but he missed that season's League Cup Final defeat by his future club Aston Villa because he had already played in the competition for the Potters.

He spent two and a half injury-dogged years at Goodison Park, leaving Merseyside for Villa Park in a £225,000 deal in September 1979. Sadly, he struggled with his fitness once again and in the end was forced to take off his boots after one season under Ron Saunders's management, just as Villa were gearing themselves up for a shot at the League title, which they won in 1981.

Despite qualifying as a senior coach, after quitting the game Mike went into farming in North Staffordshire before becoming manager of non-League side Leek Town in July 1981, switching to Northwich Victoria in the same capacity for the 1982–83 season. In July 1986 he was appointed coach by Port Vale and moved up the ladder to become head coach in December 1987, retaining that position for five years. Thereafter he was an FA coach in the North East, a development officer for the FA and briefly a coach in Kuwait prior to returning to the UK in 1994 as manager of Chester City. He was in charge there for just one season before going back to his former club, Port Vale, as youth-team coach in 1995, staying until 1999.

Mike enjoyed his time as a non-League manager and also to a degree at Chester, but it was in the field of coaching that he excelled, nurturing along such stars as striker Jermaine Defoe and wingers Aaron Lennon and Stewart Downing, all of whom went on to play for England at senior level. He also taught FA coaching courses at a North Warwickshire College in Nuneaton before becoming head of youth coaching at Championship side Plymouth Argyle in February 2007.

Mike's younger brother, Mel, played for Stoke City, Hereford United, and Wrexham while his nephew, Shaun Pejic, the son of Mel, is currently with Wrexham, managed by former Potter Denis Smith, an ex-teammate of Mike's.

Don Ratcliffe

Born: 13 November 1934, Newcastle-under-Lyme

Stoke City record:
Appearances: League 238, FA Cup 18, League Cup 4
Goals: League 18, FA Cup 3
Debut: League, 25 December 1954 v Bury (h) won 3–2

Also played for: Middlesbrough, Darlington, Crewe Alexandra, Northwich Victoria

Don Ratcliffe was a local lad who joined Stoke City straight from school as an amateur in April 1950 and turned professional in November 1951.

Nurtured through the junior and reserve teams, he was understudy to Johnny Malkin for a while before making his League debut at outside-right against Bury in a Second Division match at the Victoria Ground on Christmas Day 1954, having a hand in one of Johnny King's hat-trick goals in a 3–2 win before 18,312 fans.

Don made 10 more first-team appearances that season, six at inside-left as partner to Harry Oscroft. He also scored his first goals at senior level, finding the net in the second and fourth games of five tough third-round FA Cup matches against Bury.

The following term Don was called into action on eight occasions, and he played only once in 1956–57, taking over on the left wing in a 1–1 home draw with Doncaster Rovers. In 1957–58 he established himself as a regular in the first XI by making 33 appearances, 31 in the League, while lining up in both wing-half positions and on both wings.

In 1958–59 Potters manager Frank Taylor used six players in the outside-right position, Don wearing the number-seven shirt 10 times and the number-11 jersey on five occasions. A truly versatile footballer, he could play anywhere and always gave a good account of himself.

In 1959–60, when he shared the wing-half positions with Bill Asprey and Bobby Cairns, Don scored once in 31 League appearances, but the following season he had his best in Stoke City's red-and-white colours, taking the field in all but one of the club's 49 competitive games. The only fixture he missed was the home League clash with Brighton and Hove Albion in late April.

Stoke's best performance that season came in mid-December when they thrashed hapless Plymouth Argyle 9–0 at the Victoria Ground. Don was outstanding that afternoon and scored twice while having a hand in four other goals as the Pilgrims were torn apart.

Dan occupied both wing positions in 1961–62, adding a further 43 senior appearances to his overall tally, and was an ever present in 1962–63 when the Potters won the Second Division Championship and so regained top-flight status for the first time since 1953.

With Stanley Matthews on the right wing, Don played at inside-left and outside-left and four of his five League goals were all-important in their own right. He netted at a crucial time in the 6–3 home win over Charlton Athletic, won the game at Plymouth, started the ball rolling in a 3–1 home success over Rotherham United and took the pressure off with a second goal in a 3–0 victory at Portsmouth.

After such an excellent medal-winning campaign, Don started the 1963–64 season impressively enough as the Potters attempted to make an impact among the big boys, but then, seemingly out of the blue, Middlesbrough manager Raich Carter enquired about his availability and in a matter of days Don was transferred to the Ayresome Park club for a fee of £30,000.

He had given the supporters an enormous amount of pleasure and had been a totally dedicated footballer for the club, scoring 22 goals in 260 appearances.

Don played in 71 competitive games for Boro, scoring three goals before moving to Darlington in February 1966. He did well at The Feethams for two years, netting a further 12 goals in 85 League outings up to January 1968, when he moved closer to his Stoke roots by signing for Crewe Alexandra. At Gresty Road he added two goals and 50 appearances to his career record before switching to Northwich Victoria in May 1969, eventually retiring in 1971, aged 36.

Don's League career spanned 16 years, during which time he scored 40 goals in 475 club appearances.

John Ritchie

Born:	12 July 1941, Kettering, Northamptonshire
Died:	23 February 2007, Stoke-on-Trent

Stoke City record:

Appearances:	League 261+9, FA Cup 27, League Cup 37+1, others 7+1
Goals:	League 135, FA Cup 15, League Cup 18, others 3
Debut:	League, 13 April 1963 v Cardiff City (h) won 1–0

Also played for: Kettering Town, Sheffield Wednesday and Stafford Rangers

Writing John Ritchie's obituary in *The Times*, soccer reporter and columnist Brian Glanville said 'If there was ever an *annus mirabilis* both for John Ritchie and his club Stoke City, it was the 1971–72 season, when they won the Football League Cup and reached the semi-finals of the FA Cup, only to go out to Arsenal in a replay.'

That League Cup triumph at Wembley is the only major competition Stoke have won so far, despite their long history and a galaxy of stars, among them the incomparable Stanley Matthews, centre-forward Freddie Steele, elegant centre-half Neil Franklin and England goalkeeper Gordon Banks.

John, who died in 2007 at the age of 65 after a long illness, was a typical English centre-forward, 6ft tall, 12st in weight, strong on the ground, powerful in the air and certainly a player defenders found hard to handle. In June 1962, he was a member of a Stoke City team cleverly put together by genial manager Tony Waddington, who specialised in reinvigorating the careers of veteran players. One such player was the 35-year-old George Eastham, in his heyday an electric inside-forward with England, Newcastle United and Arsenal, who scored a rare goal in that League Cup Final, Stoke's second against the favourites, Chelsea. Big John had much to do with it. Elusive Irish-born winger Terry Conroy sold his marker a dummy out on the left at a time when Chelsea, with the score at 1–1, were calling the tune. When Conroy crossed, John expertly headed the ball back to Jimmy Greenhoff, whose fierce drive brought a superb save from Peter Bonetti. He could not hold the ball and Eastham prodded it home.

John had many other splendid moments that season, in which he claimed 12 goals in the League, four in the League Cup and two in the FA Cup to finish as leading scorer. This excellent campaign came during his second spell with Stoke.

John initially joined the Potters from his local club, Kettering Town, in June 1962 for just £2,500, and made his debut in 1962–63, Stoke's promotion season from the Second Division. He appeared in 135 competitive games and struck 81 goals before joining Sheffield Wednesday for £80,000 in November 1966. He then added a further 45 goals in 106 senior appearances with the Owls before rejoining Stoke in July 1969 for £25,000.

To be in an attack alongside Greenhoff, Conroy, Eastham and Peter Dobing was surely a centre-forward's dream, and John rose to the occasion. Greenhoff and Dobing were his main strike partners, Conroy the wide man who regularly delivered the perfect cross aimed for John's head, and Eastham the creator, the architect in midfield who fed his winger and the front men with measured passes.

After spending a total of 10 years with the Potters, John's senior career effectively came to an end in September 1974 when, during a League game at Ipswich Town, he was involved in a collision with rugged defender Kevin Beattie. John severely fractured his right leg, and although he recovered from that devastating blow, he never played at a high level again. He did assist non-League Stafford Rangers briefly before announcing his retirement for good in January 1976.

He netted 171 goals for Stoke in 343 appearances and is currently the highest League and Cup goalscorer in the club's history. One interesting thing that happened to John as a 'Stokie' came during a UEFA Cup game in Germany against FC Kaiserslautern in September 1972. As a substitute, he took the field but was sent off after just 29 seconds without ever touching the ball, dismissed for throwing a punch at an opponent.

Appropriately, John ran a pottery business in Stoke-on-Trent after his footballing days were over. He is survived by his wife Shirley, two sons and a daughter.

Bill Robertson

Born:	25 March 1923, Crowthorne, near Reading
Died:	c.1973, south London

Stoke City record:

Appearances:	League 238, FA Cup 12
Debut:	League, 23 August 1952 v Manchester City (h) won 2–1
Also played for:	Crowthorne Boys Club, Camberley ATC, Chelsea, Birmingham City

Bill Robertson, standing 6ft 1in tall and weighing around 14st, was a very efficient goalscoring centre-forward with the Crowthorne Boys Club before joining the forces at the age of 15. He continued to lead the attack with confidence when playing for Camberley Auxiliary Training Corps, scoring plenty of goals and helping them win the Aldershot Minor League Championship in his first season.

At the age of 20, Bill was asked to take over in goal in an emergency. The match in question was a Cup semi-final in March 1943. He went out and produced an excellent display, so much so that he was chosen in the same position the two following weeks and played in the Final, which unfortunately his team lost. Bill never looked back after that and went on to have a decent career.

On his demobilisation in October 1945, Bill was signed as a full-time professional by Chelsea, having been spotted playing for RAF Lossiemouth, linking up with another goalkeeper with exactly the same name.

Acting as first reserve to Harry Medhurst, Bill remained at Stamford Bridge until November 1948, when he moved to newly promoted Birmingham City for £2,500 having appeared in 43 senior games for the London club, 27 of them in the Football League (South). His chances were limited at St Andrews because of the form of Gil Merrick, and he managed only three competitive appearances for Blues (in almost four years). Bill transferred to Stoke City for a fee of £8,000 in June 1952, becoming the first player to be signed by the Potters' new manager, Frank Taylor.

Bill went on to have eight excellent seasons under Taylor at the Victoria Ground, overcoming a fractured leg to go on and amass exactly 250 appearances between the posts. In fact, his tally of senior appearances for the Potters remained a club record for a goalkeeper until Peter Fox surpassed it in 1984.

A fine shot-stopper with good reflexes, and a 'keeper who commanded his area with authority, Bill took over from Dennis Herod and made his senior debut for Stoke on the opening day of the 1952–53 season at home to Manchester City. He did very well, pulled off several smart saves and helped the Potters register a 2–1 victory in front of 35,000 fans. However, in the return fixture with City at Maine Road in December, Bill broke his right leg when he ran out of his area to thwart an attack. Bill, who had made 19 appearances during the first half of that season, was replaced by Herod, and before the campaign was over Frank Elliott had also been used between the posts.

It was quite some time before Bill regained full fitness and, after long, tedious periods in the treatment room, on the walking machine and under the physio's lamp, he eventually returned to first-team action against Rotherham United at Millmoor in September 1953, taking over from Elliott. He remained Stoke City's first-choice goalkeeper until September 1957, appearing in every game (43 in all) during the 1956–57 season.

Bill's last two seasons with the Potters earned him a further 52 appearances and in May 1960, at the age of 37, he reluctantly announced his retirement from competitive football, mainly due to a pain in his previously fractured leg. He was effectively replaced in the Stoke City goal by Irish international Jimmy O'Neill and, in fact, during his time at the Victoria Ground (1952–60) Bill was one of five goalkeepers used by manager Frank Taylor. He had a 23 per cent record for keeping clean sheets (63 out of his 250 starts).

After quitting football Bill ran a successful newsagents in Bucknall, Stoke-on-Trent, for three years and in 1963 returned to London, where he remained for the rest of his life.

Jimmy Robertson

Born: 17 December 1944, Cardonald, Glasgow

Stoke City record:

Appearances: League 99+15, FA Cup 9, League Cup 8+1, others 5+2
Goals: League 12, League Cup 2
Debut: League, 12 August 1972, Crystal Palace (h) won 2–0

Also played for: Middlesbrough (trialist), Celtic (amateur), Cowdenbeath, St
                 Mirren, Tottenham Hotspur, Arsenal, Seattle Sounders, Walsall,
                 Crewe Alexandra, Scotland (4 Under-23 and 1 full caps)

Glasgow-born winger Jimmy Robertson was a sound investment who always paid dividends. His 19-year career as a professional began in the less salubrious surroundings of Cowdenbeath, and because he was under 17 Jimmy was forced to sign amateur forms for the unfashionable Scottish club, having earlier had unsuccessful spells with both Middlesbrough (as a schoolboy trialist) and Celtic (as a part-timer).

He made rapid progress with Cowdenbeath, won Scottish Youth and amateur caps, and in April 1962 was taken on as a full-time professional by St Mirren. He spent two years at Love Street, and represented his country at Under-23 level before switching his allegiance to Tottenham Hotspur, signed by manager Bill Nicholson for a bargain fee of just £25,000 in March 1964.

He went straight into the Spurs forward line, lining up on the left wing with Les Allen as his inside partner at Anfield. Later in the season he played with Jimmy Greaves and Bobby Smith, and in 1964–65 his fellow forwards included Alan Gilzean, Cliff Jones and Terry Dyson, with Alan Mullery and Maurice Norman behind him and Pat Jennings in goal.

Spurs were a useful side, and in 1967 they reached the FA Cup final, Jimmy having the pleasure of scoring the first goal in a 2–1 win over Chelsea.

'Alan Mullery had a shot which deflected off a defender. The ball fell to me and I simply put it into the net from close range. It just seems like it happened yesterday!' recalls Jimmy.

Jimmy admitted that he made the worst mistake of his career a year later when he left White Hart Lane and moved across London to neighbours Arsenal, in an exchange deal involving David Jenkins. He had scored 43 goals in 215 games for Spurs, gained further under-23 honours and played in one full international versus Wales in 1965.

He said 'Going to Highbury seemed like a great move at the time, but very few players had switched between the two clubs and I never really settled in with the Gunners.'

He managed to score eight goals in 59 outings for Arsenal, but after falling out with boss Bertie Mee he was transferred to Ipswich Town for £50,000 in March 1970.

He spent a little over two seasons at Portman Road, making 98 appearances and netting 12 goals before leaving East Anglia for the Potteries in June 1972, Stoke manager Tony Waddington paying only

£10,000 for his services. Jimmy has called Stoke his home ever since.

He gave the Potters five years' excellent service, appearing in almost 140 competitive games and notching 14 goals. He partnered Jimmy Greenhoff on the right wing in his first two seasons but was sidelined through injury in 1974–75 and again during the early part of 1975–76. On his return he linked up again with Greenhoff, with Welsh international John Mahoney backing up both players from the right-half position.

In the summer of 1976 he assisted the NASL club Seattle Sounders, but injuries affected his game again during the 1976–77 season and he made only 14 League appearances as Stoke slipped out of the top flight. After a second spell with the Sounders, Jimmy moved to Walsall in September 1977 and 12 months later joined Crewe Alexandra, retiring in May 1979.

He subsequently worked for a computer company before holding the purse strings in his own company, Gillen Financial Services, based in Hanley, Stoke-on-Trent.

Jimmy, married with two daughters, has not severed links with the game. He still attends matches at Stoke and Crewe, and even travels to Vale Park occasionally, but nowadays his greatest love is golf. He is pretty nifty with the small ball, playing off a handicap of seven at the Newcastle-under-Lyme club. He said: 'I've won more trophies playing golf than I did playing football.'

Leigh Richmond Roose, MM

Born: 27 November 1877, Holt, near Wrexham
Died: 7 October 1916, France

Stoke City record:

Appearances: League 147, FA Cup 12
Debut: League, 19 October 1901 v Blackburn Rovers (h) drew 2–2

Also played for: UCW Aberystwyth, Aberystwyth Town, Druids, London Welsh, Everton, Celtic, Sunderland, Port Vale (guest), Huddersfield Town, Aston Villa, Woolwich Arsenal, Llandudno Town, Wales (24 full caps)

Goalkeeper 'Mond' Roose played League football from 1901 until 1912. An amateur playing against professionals, he was regarded as one of the best players in his position.

The son of a Presbyterian minister, he was educated at Holt Academy and the University of Wales, and after graduating studied medicine at King's College Hospital but never qualified as a doctor. He began with Aberystwyth Town, for whom he made 58 appearances, gaining a Welsh Cup-winners' medal in 1900 against his future club, Druids.

Signed by Stoke in October 1901, Mond appeared in 159 games in two spells for the Potters, keeping 40 clean sheets. His first spell ended in November 1904 when he moved to Everton and his second ran from September 1905 to September 1907, when he transferred to Celtic. Unfortunately, a broken wrist ended his career at the Victoria Ground.

Mond punctuated his spells at Stoke with 24 appearances for Everton and afterwards played 99 times for Sunderland, helping the Wearsiders twice finish runners-up in Division One while almost single-handedly saving them from relegation in 1908.

When he left Sunderland in 1910 (after sustaining a second broken wrist) there was a call for his services to be recognised with a testimonial, but being an amateur this could not be granted and instead he was presented with an illuminated address.

During his career, Mond made over 300 appearances, charging most of his clubs handsomely for his expenses. As a 'Stokie', he missed a train from London to Birmingham for a game against Villa in 1905. At the time, railway companies kept private trains ready for hire by wealthy travellers. Mond engaged such a train, which took him all the way to Birmingham at a cost of 5s (25p) a mile plus the ordinary fare. He then arranged for the £31 bill – a fortune in those days – to be sent to his club. And as a Sunderland player he once submitted a claim for 'Using the toilet (twice)...2d (1p)'.

Mond won 24 caps for Wales – his first versus Ireland in 1900, his last against Scotland in 1911. He was one of Wales' key players when the team won the Home Championship for the first time in 1907.

The *Athletic Times* described him as being 'dexterous though daring, valiant though volatile'. And Geraint Jenkins, an Aberystwyth historian, said he boasted 'sharp eyesight, startling reflexes, competitive instinct and reckless bravery'.

In April 1910, Mond guested with Herbert Chapman for Port Vale against Stoke reserves in a match that would decide the North Staffordshire & District League title. Not only did he insist on playing against his former club wearing his old Stoke jersey, but he also aroused the ire of 7,000 spectators with his breathtaking play. He saved every shot with such arrogant ease that the furious crowd spilled onto the pitch and only the intervention of the police saved him from a ducking in the River Trent. Stoke's ground was closed for the first fortnight of 1910–11.

In March 1909 Mond travelled with Wales to play Ireland. Arriving at Liverpool station with one hand heavily bandaged, he told the press that he had broken two fingers but would still play. Later his Welsh teammate Billy Meredith, suspecting trickery, peered through the keyhole of Mond's Belfast hotel room door and saw him remove the bandage and wiggle his fingers with no sign of discomfort. News of Mond's injury spread quickly and a huge crowd assembled in the hope of witnessing an Irish victory. Instead Wales won 3–2 and Mond played brilliantly.

Mond joined the army as a private in 1916 and served on the Western Front, where his goalkeeping abilities resulted in him becoming a noted grenade thrower. He was awarded the Military Medal for his bravery on his first mission, but soon after his promotion to the rank of lance corporal he was killed at the Battle of the Somme.

Billy Rowley

Born:	12 July 1865, Hanley, Stoke-on-Trent
Died:	12 June 1939, United States of America

Stoke City record:

Appearances:	League 124, FA Cup 15
Debut:	FA Cup, 30 October 1886 v Caernarvon Wanderers (h) won 10–1

Also played for: Hanley Orion, Burslem Port Vale, Leicester Fosse, England (2 full caps)

Goalkeeper William Spencer Rowley played in Stoke's first-ever League game against West Bromwich Albion in September 1888 and also became the club's first England goalkeeper when he appeared against Ireland at Anfield in March 1889, a game the English won 6–1.

Billy had two spells with the Potters and overall made 139 competitive appearances as well as starring in over 100 other games (friendlies and local Cup competitions).

Born in the Potteries and originally a centre-forward with Hanley Orion, he joined Stoke first time round in August 1883. Successfully switching his duties from goalscoring to goalkeeping, he stayed with the club for barely a year, transferring his allegiance to Burslem Port Vale in April 1884. He made 66 first-team appearances for the Valiants, helping them share the North Staffordshire Charity Cup and win the Burslem Charity Cup in 1885. In fact, he scored in the Final of the latter competition, when Ironbridge were hammered 12–0. Vale were so much on top that he ventured upfield and thumped the ball between the posts for his side's 10th goal.

A fractured rib, suffered against Stoke in a friendly match in May 1886, kept him out of work for four months. However, while recovering from this injury he chose to return to the Victoria Ground in August 1886, despite having signed a binding contract to play for the Vale. Centre-half George Bateman joined Stoke with him. In November 1886 Vale took the Stoke club to Burslem County Court over the incident. They won the case and Stoke were ordered to pay £20 to a local charity.

At that point Stoke sent both players (Billy and George) back to the Vale but then, surprisingly, there was another twist to this bizarre affair. The following month Vale agreed to release the same two players from their contracts, allowing them to officially sign for the Potters, thus Billy started a second term with the club.

He had made his first-class debut for the Potters in an FA Cup qualifying game against Caernarvon Wanderers at home in October 1886. He had hardly anything to do during the whole game as the Potters raced to a comprehensive 10–1 win.

Billy's superb displays between the posts during the late 1880s resulted in him winning numerous representative honours for Staffordshire. He later played for the Football League XI (1892–93) and starred in four international trials. The last, in March 1892, clinched him his second full cap, which also came against Ireland in Belfast, when the two full-backs in front of him were his Stoke colleagues Tommy Clare and Alf Underwood. This time England won 2–0.

Billy was Stoke's first-choice goalkeeper for four seasons but injuries limited him to six appearances in 1890–91 when the team won the Football Alliance Championship, after being relegated from the Football League 12 months earlier. He was back to full fitness come the start of the 1891–92 campaign, and he went on to serve the club until the summer of 1897, when he quit playing to concentrate on his job as the club's secretary-manager, a position he accepted in May 1895. He was technically an amateur at this stage of his career having relinquished professional status, and this allowed him to take the office job while still an active player.

As Stoke's boss, Billy was involved in more controversy in August 1898 when he transferred himself to Leicester Fosse, who paid a small signing-on fee for his signature. He made only one senior appearance for Leicester before he and the secretary of Leicester, Mr W.D. Clark, were brought before the FA. Fosse were fined £10 and both Billy and his counterpart (Clark) were suspended for 12 months for 'such unethical practice'.

Billy never returned to football, retiring to become a licensee in Stoke-on-Trent before immigrating to the US, where he died a month before his 74th birthday.

Tommy Sale

Born:	30 April 1910, Stoke-on-Trent
Died:	10 November 1990

Stoke City record:

Appearances:	League 204, FA Cup 19, wartime 260
Goals:	League 98, FA Cup 5, wartime 179
Debut:	League, 25 December 1933 v Bradford City (a) drew 2–2

Also played for: Stoke St Peter's, Blackburn Rovers, Northwich Victoria, Hednesford Town

Tommy Sale was an out-and-out striker, an inside or centre-forward who had two spells with his home-town club, Stoke City, accumulating a grand total of 483 first-team appearances and 282 goals, of which 179 came in 260 World War Two matches. He was also a penalty expert and it is on record that he missed only once from the spot throughout his career. In between his spells with the Potters he had a two-year stint with Blackburn Rovers and later on in his career, as his legs started to feel the pain, he assisted two non-league clubs, Northwich Victoria and Hednesford Town.

As a 14-year-old, Tommy worked in a pottery factory. In conjunction with his work, he played football at weekends for Stoke St Peter's (a youth side officially linked with Stoke City). His performances attracted the attention of Potters manager Tom Mather and in August 1929, at the age of 19, he was registered as an amateur with the club.

In May 1930 Tommy was given a professional contract and seven months later, on Christmas Day, he made his League debut at inside-left in a 2-2 draw at Bradford City.

By the 1932-33 season, Tommy had established himself as a prominent member of the Potters' first team, and he helped them win the Second Division by notching 11 goals in 21 League appearances as part of a tremendous three-pronged scoring attack with centre-forward Joe Mawson and left-winger Joe Johnson.

During the following two seasons, Tommy was the club's leading scorer. He netted 17 times in the 1933-34 season, in which Stoke finished 12th in the First Division, and followed up with 24 (all in the League) in 1934-35, when the Potters edged up to 10th place.

Bob McGrory, Mather's successor as Stoke manager, sold Tommy to Blackburn Rovers in March 1936 for the sum of £6,000. This surprised supporters at the time, but McGrory had confidence in a young Freddie Steele, who he had earmarked as a potential replacement.

Tommy spent exactly two years at Ewood Park before returning to the Victoria Ground in March 1938 – this after Rovers had been relegated to the Second Division in bottom spot at the end of the 1935-36 season, finished a disappointing 12th in 1936-37 and were hovering too near the danger zone at the time of his departure.

Re-signed, initially as cover for the injured Steele, Tommy scored five goals in three games as he set about regaining his place in the first team, and he duly consolidated his position by netting another 18 goals in the 1938-39 campaign.

Unfortunately, the 1939-40 season was suspended due to the outbreak of World War Two, but that didn't stop Tommy from enjoying his football – and scoring goals. He continued his explosive goal-grabbing with a haul of 17 (in all competitions) in 1940-41, 56 in 1941-42 (including a double hat-trick versus Walsall in January), 10 more in 1942-43, 30 in 1943-44 and another 34 in 1944-45.

His goals dried up somewhat in the transitional season of 1945-46, when he claimed only eight. This, in fact, turned out to be Tommy's last season as a top-line footballer. Tommy's final appearance in a Stoke City shirt came on 8 April 1946, at the age of 35, when he lined up in a League North game against Sheffield United at the Victoria Ground. A crowd of just 9,000 turned out to see the Potters lose 3-0 but, more importantly, those present said farewell to a great goalscorer.

Tommy remained at the club for another year before transferring to Northwich Victoria in June 1947. He switched to Hednesford Town in August 1948, finally announcing his retirement in July 1949, aged 39.

Lee Sandford

Born:	22 April 1968, Basingstoke, Hampshire

Stoke City record:

Appearances:	League 209+3, FA Cup 14, League Cup 16, others 27
Goals:	League 8, FA Cup 2, others 4
Debut:	League, 26 December 1989 v Newcastle United (h) won 2–1

Also played for: Portsmouth, Sheffield United, Reading

Capped by England at Schoolboy and Youth levels, Lee Sandford served his apprenticeship with Portsmouth before making his League debut as a substitute left-back against Millwall in October 1985. Two months later he turned professional, gained a regular place in the first team at Fratton Park and was named the club's Player of the Month in September 1987 after scoring the first goal of his career in a 2–1 home win over Wimbledon.

Out of the first team for five months with a spinal injury, he returned to action in February 1988 and two months later found himself keeping goal just two minutes into a League match against Wimbledon, when he deputised for Alan Knight who went off with a facial injury. He did well and helped his side earn a point from a 2–2 draw.

Lee took his tally of competitive appearances with Pompey to a creditable 94 before transferring to Stoke City for £137,500 three days before Christmas 1989.

Tall, strong in the tackle and able to defend and attack, Lee went on to give the Potters excellent service for six and a half seasons, during which time he amassed a splendid record of 269 senior appearances and 14 goals. He was in the Potters' Autoglass Trophy-winning team against Stockport County at Wembley in 1992 and their Second Division Championship-winning side the following season.

Starting off wearing the number-11 shirt and playing wide left in midfield in front of Cliff Carr, Lee made an impressive debut against Newcastle United

at the Victoria Ground on Boxing Day 1989. As the campaign progressed he occupied the centre-half, left-half and left-back positions and ended his first half-season with 24 appearances to his name and two goals, both of which were to no avail as the Potters lost 2–1 against Oxford United and Leicester City. Unfortunately, he also tasted relegation as Stoke slipped into the Third Division for the first time since season 1926–27.

In 1990–91 Lee played mostly alongside Noel Blake in the centre of the Stoke back four, with former England international left-back Derek Statham behind him and Paul Ware, Vince Hilaire and Brian Rice occupying the left side of midfield.

Lee made 40 appearances that term and scored three goals, including a point-saver against Brentford and the winner in a first-round FA Cup replay over non-League side Telford United.

During season 1991–92, when over 48,000 fans saw the Potters win at Wembley (a day Lee will never forget) he played at left-back and left-half and amassed 53 appearances, netting three goals, all of them in the Autoglass Trophy competition. The first two came in the preliminary round victory over Walsall, while his other helped salvage a first-leg semi-final 3–3 draw with Peterborough United.

Lee missed just four League games in 1992–93 as Stoke won the newly formed Second Division title, and was absent from the same number the following season when he scored an extra-special winning goal in a 2–1 Boxing Day victory over Birmingham City at the Victoria Ground.

Over the next two seasons Lee's form was superb. He made almost 100 appearances and was an ever present (for the first time in his career) in 1995–96. At that point he was being pursued by several other clubs and it came as no surprise when, in July 1996, former Stoke City favourite Howard Kendall signed him for Sheffield United for a fee of £500,000.

Lee continued to perform with competence and commitment for the Blades and added almost 60 more appearances to his overall tally, as well as having a loan spell with Reading (September–October 1997). He announced his retirement from competitive League football in May 1998, shortly after Sheffield United lost in the First Division Play-off semi-final to Sunderland.

In his lengthy and interesting career Lee made 478 League and Cup appearances and scored 18 goals.

Joey Schofield

Born:	1 January 1871, Hanley, Stoke-on-Trent
Died:	29 September 1929, Hartshill, Stoke-on-Trent

Stoke City record:

Appearances:	League 204, FA Cup 22, others 4
Goals:	League 84, FA Cup 8, others 2
Debut:	League, 10 October 1891 v Burnley (h) won 3–0

Also played for: England (3 full caps)

A speedy and extremely clever footballer, Joey Schofield was the perfect gentleman on and off the pitch and had few peers at outside-left in the 1890s. Lightly built, he enjoyed running at his opponent and regularly got the upper hand. He could cross a ball on the run, but if given time and space he would often stop before the byline and then deliver the ball into the danger zone with deliberate and measured perfection.

A keen sportsman at Hanley Hope Sunday School, Joey qualified as a maths and English teacher at Broom Street School in Hanley and was also employed as a Poor Law official. At the age of 20 he joined the Potters as a part-time professional in August 1891, choosing this sort of agreement owing to his educational profession. He spent eight excellent seasons at the Victoria Ground before retiring (through injury) in April 1899.

He scored on his senior debut for the club in a 3–0 home League win over Burnley as a centre-forward and ended his first season of competitive football with 12 goals (eight in the League, four in the FA Cup) in 20 appearances. He also gained the first of three full caps for England, starring in a 2–0 win over Wales at Wrexham when he partnered Rupert Sandilands on the left-wing.

In 1892–93 he finished up as Stoke's leading scorer with 13 goals, which included a terrific hat-trick in a 3–3 draw with Blackburn Rovers at Ewood Park, and he won his second international cap, scoring in a comprehensive 6–0 victory over the Welsh at the Victoria Ground in front of 10,000 spectators. Stoke's Tommy Clare also played in this game. He was also twice called up to represent the Football League against teams from the Scottish and Irish Leagues.

Twelve months on, in 1893–94, he was once again the Potters' top marksman with a total of 18 goals in all competitions, and regarded as one of the finest outside-lefts in the game – but he couldn't get into the England side owing to the form of Sheffield Wednesday's Fred Spiksley.

Joey had to wait until March 1895 before gaining his third cap and this time he was outstanding, having a hand in four of the goals in England's emphatic 9–0 win over Ireland at The County Cricket Club ground, Derby. That season (1894–95) Joey was joint-top scorer (with Bill Dickson) on 13 goals, and in 1895–96 he netted nine, three of them in a 6–1 home League victory over Small Heath when he also missed a penalty.

Joey's last three seasons yielded a further 29 goals in 83 outings, bringing his overall career figures for Stoke to 94 goals in 230 senior appearances. On his retirement at the age of 28 (due to ill heath) he joined the club's office staff and in 1908, when the club slipped into the Birmingham and District League, he became a director, taking over as secretary-manager of the Potters in 1915, a position he held until shortly after Christmas 1918.

In January 1919 Joey moved across the city to take over as secretary of Stoke's arch-rivals Port Vale, who also gave him team management responsibilities before upgrading him to full-time secretary-manager in March 1920.

A man of well-balanced judgement, he had the knack of discovering and developing promising young players, and in time became the players' 'friend, confidant and counsellor'. He guided Vale to victory in the North Staffordshire Infirmary Cup Finals of 1920 and 1922 and in between times sold the fans' favourite player Bobby Blood to West Bromwich Albion for a club record £4,000. In June 1923 he was fined £25 for his involvement in the payment of illegal bonuses to no fewer than 17 players!

After that upheaval, in March 1927 Joey was appointed full-time team manager of the Valiants. Unfortunately, two years later he was taken ill and admitted to hospital. He never recovered and sadly died in Hartshill in September 1929 with his team (Port Vale) sitting on top of the Third Division North table and Stoke one division higher.

Harry Sellars

Born:	9 April 1902, Beamish, County Durham
Died:	30 December 1978, Stoke-on-Trent

Stoke City record:

Appearances:	League 369, FA Cup 25
Goals:	League 20, FA Cup 1
Debut:	League, 26 January 1924 v Clapton Orient (a) won 2–0

Also played for: Ledgate Park FC, Port Vale, Drumcondra (player-manager)

When Harry moved south to join Stoke from Ledgate Park in December 1923 it was the start of a long association for the Sellars family at the Victoria Ground.

Aged 21 at the time and able to play in both wing-half positions as well as inside-left, he remained with the club until July 1937 (14 years) while his son, Johnny, was a player at the Victoria Ground from 1942 until 1959 (17 years).

Harry was a well-built footballer, strong in the tackle, a fine passer of the ball and a terrific club man who battled through every game as if it was a Cup Final.

A former miner in a Durham coalfield, Harry scored on his League debut for the Potters in a 2–0 home win over Clapton Orient on a bitterly cold winter's afternoon in late January 1924. He was introduced into the first team by manager Tom Mather at a time when a replacement was required for the injured Johnny Eyres.

Harry played in the next game (versus Stockport County) and in the last six, netting both goals in a 2–0 home win over Barnsley. The following season he was called into action nine times, making his first appearance in the FA Cup when Stoke lost 3–0 to Leicester City.

In 1925–26 he played in 13 League games (scoring two goals) before gaining a regular place in the team at right-half in 1926–27. The season ended in glory for Harry and the team, with the Third Division North Championship trophy being presented to skipper Bob McGrory.

Harry lined up in 33 League and Cup games that term and 37 in 1927–28 as the Potters consolidated themselves in Division Two. Absent just twice in 1928–29 when he was the team's permanent left-half, Harry came very close to selection for the Football League side after producing some fine displays, continuing to do so in 1929–30 when he again missed only two fixtures.

Holding his position confidently and virtually unchallenged, despite the fact that there were some very capable reserves ready to step forward, Harry reached the personal milestone of 200 first-team appearances for Stoke away to Bristol City in December 1930. After being an ever present for the first time in his career in 1931–32, the following season he celebrated with his teammates when Stoke City won the Second Division Championship and so regained their top-flight status after an absence of 10 years.

Harry made 39 League appearances in 1932–33 and netted two goals, his first being the winner at Burnley (2–1) and his second coming in a healthy 4–0 home win over Bradford Park Avenue a week later.

Continuing to hold his form and his place in the first team, Harry reached the milestone of 300 appearances for the club towards the end of that 1932–33 campaign, and after being appointed as assistant manager to McGrory he went on to take his final tally to 394 before transferring to neighbours Port Vale in July 1937. His last game for the Potters was against Arsenal at home in September 1935, when over 45,000 fans saw the Gunners win 3–0.

Surprisingly, he never made the Valiants' first team and in season 1939–40 he opted for a change of lifestyle and scenery by becoming player-manager of the Irish club Drumcondra, a position he held for just one season.

He retired from football during the war and returned to Stoke-on-Trent to watch his son, Johnny, make the grade as a professional footballer with the Potters, thus carrying on the family's reputation of producing high-quality, dedicated players. Between them, father and son spent a total of 31 years with Stoke City football club, making a combined total of 852 first-team appearances between them.

Johnny Sellars

Born: 28 April 1924, Trent Vale, Stoke-on-Trent
Died: April 1985, Stoke-on-Trent

Stoke City record:
Appearances: League 384, FA Cup 29, wartime 45
Goals: League 14, FA Cup 1, wartime 13
Debut: Wartime, 17 April 1943 v Derby County (a) lost 2–1
               League, 1 February 1947 v Preston North End (h) won 5–0

Signed by Stoke City on the recommendation of his father, Harry, in March 1943 as a promising 16-year-old, Johnny Sellars made his first appearance in the senior side 11 days before his 17th birthday in the Football League North (second period) game away to Derby County in front of 5,000 spectators.

He went on to play in 45 competitive matches during the wartime period, having his best spells in the first team in seasons 1944–45 (five goals) and 1945–46 (seven goals).

After the resumption of peacetime football, he finally claimed a regular place in the Potters' senior side halfway through the 1946–47 campaign, when he took over the right-half position from Frank Mountford. He did very well, held his position without trouble and went on an unbroken run of 18 matches from February through to mid-June, the season having been extended due to the severe arctic weather conditions that gripped the country in the winter. He also scored two goals in successive weeks, both at the Victoria Ground, in excellent wins over Chelsea (6–1) and Arsenal (3–1).

Retaining his place in the team for the start of the 1947–48 season, he was used as a centre-forward in five games during late October and November and then as a right-winger in eight fixtures either side of Christmas and the New Year, but he was quickly moved back into his favourite half-back position, albeit on the left-hand side. He remained there for virtually the next two seasons before switching over to the right to accommodate Jock Kirton.

In 1948–49 Johnny was an ever present, and in 1949–50 he missed only two League games versus Manchester United and Chelsea, while in 1950–51 he was absent for just one, sitting out the 1–1 draw at Derby. Around that period he had two decent runs in the team, making 61 consecutive appearances between March 1948 and September 1949 and another 91 between October 1949 and December 1950.

Injury caused Johnny to miss the first 14 weeks of the 1951–52 League programme, and during the second half of the campaign he played at right-back, right-half, left-half, inside-right and centre-forward, proving what a versatile and invaluable player he was.

From August 1953 through to April 1958 Johnny played some exceptionally fine football, missing matches only through injury and illness, although at times he did come under pressure from the likes of Alan Martin, Bill Asprey and Bobby Cairns. When fit and available, he tended to be one of the first names on manager Frank Taylor's team sheet.

Not one of the club's greatest-ever scoring half-backs, Johnny managed only 15 goals at top-class level for the Potters. He had his best net-bulging campaign in 1951–52, weighing in with four goals, including a brace (one of them from the penalty spot) in a spirited 2–1 home win over high-riding Arsenal in December. He was also a very useful track athlete and took part in the famous Powderhall Sprint on several occasions during the 1950s (outside the football season, of course).

Johnny began to lose some of his aggression and pace but it was a serious eye injury that eventually led to him quitting the game he loved so much. Injured in his last outing for Stoke against Huddersfield at the Victoria Ground in February 1958, his place went to his understudy, Cairns. Although he came back and played a few games in the second team, he announced his retirement from the game in May 1959, having accumulated 413 League and FA Cup appearances for the Potters.

At the time of his departure, Johnny lay fourth in the list of Stoke's all-time appearance-makers, behind Johnny McCue (542), Bob McGrory (511) and Frank Mountford (425). He has now slipped down to 12th.

Johnny divided his time between playing football and being a quality shoe designer, working for the Lotus Shoe Company in Stone, a job he continued for a while after taking off his boots.

Peter Shilton, OBE

Born: 18 September 1949, Leicester

Stoke City record:

Appearances: League 110, FA Cup 7, League Cup 4
Goals: none
Debut: League, 23 November 1974 v Wolverhampton Wanderers (a) drew 2–2

Also played for: Leicester City, Nottingham Forest, Southampton, Derby County, Plymouth Argyle, Wimbledon, Bolton Wanderers, Coventry City, West Ham United, Leyton Orient and England (3 Under-23 and 125 full caps)

At his best, Peter Shilton was an incredibly brave goalkeeper who often dived at the feet of strikers. He was commanding in the air and certainly a cut above the rest in terms of positioning. These are just some of the many skills which resulted in him becoming England's most capped footballer ever, and to be known as one of the world's best 'keepers in the 1980s.

He joined Stoke City for a world record fee for a goalkeeper of £325,000 in November 1974, having spent nine years with Leicester City. He appeared in 339 first-class matches for the Foxes, scoring one goal from a long punt downfield against Southampton at The Dell in October 1967 (won 5–1). He also helped Leicester win the Second Division title in 1971 and reach the FA Cup Final of 1969 (beaten by Manchester City).

He was indispensable during his time at the Victoria Ground, missing only two League games out of a possible 112. He kept 39 clean sheets in his total of 121 outings for the Potters, giving him a 33 per cent record of goalless matches.

When he left Filbert Street for the Victoria Ground, Peter and Liverpool's Ray Clemence were beginning a real battle as to who was rated as England's top 'keeper, and each was given his fair share of caps. In 1975, however, Clemence seemed to be getting the edge, winning eight of the nine available under manager Don Revie, though England failed to reach the 1976 European Championships during this period.

Peter did not play for England at all in 1976 and only twice in 1977. Indeed, he became so frustrated at his lack of chances that in the summer of 1976 he pulled out of the squad that was heading for the bi-centennial celebration tournament in the US and asked not to be considered again for international duty, only to reverse his decision three months later. At this juncture Clemence was in control and overtook Peter's total of senior caps as England fought in vain to reach the 1978 World Cup Finals.

Around this time, Stoke were struggling in the League, and upon relegation to the Second Division at the end of the 1976–77 season Peter asked for a transfer in the hope of reviving his England career. He was sold to Nottingham Forest for £270,000 in September 1977 and went from strength to strength after that.

He made 272 appearances for Forest, 242 for Southampton (who signed him for £300,000 in August 1982), added 211 to his tally with Derby County (whom he joined for £90,000 in July 1987), and several more while assisting Plymouth Argyle (as player-manager, March 1992–December 1994), Bolton Wanderers (March 1995) and Leyton Orient (November 1996–January 1997). He was also a non-contract player with Wimbledon, Coventry City and West Ham but failed to make any appearances for those three clubs.

Peter's honours during his career are endless. He helped Forest win the League title in 1978, the European Cup in 1979 and 1980, the European Super Cup in 1979 and the FA Charity Shield in 1978. He was also rewarded with the title of PFA Footballer of the Year in 1978, and he received the PFA Merit Award for services to football in 1990.

Peter retired in the summer of 1997 after making a then record 1,005 Football League appearances. He reached the 1,000 mark playing for Leyton Orient against Brighton & Hove Albion in December 1996.

He also played in over 100 games for five different clubs, a record that has never been beaten. He ended up with a total of 1,375 club and international appearances under his belt – a terrific record. To cap a tremendous career as a professional goalkeeper, Peter was included in the Football League 100 Legends list in 1998.

'Shilts' is now vice-president of Leicester City.

Eric Skeels

Born:	27 October 1939, Eccles, near Manchester

Stoke City record:

Appearances:	League 495+12, FA Cup 42+2, League Cup 36+2, others 2+3
Goals:	League 7
Debut:	League, 12 March 1960 v Charlton Athletic (h) lost 3–1
Also played for:	Stockport County (amateur), Seattle Sounders (NASL), Cleveland Stokers (NASL), Port Vale, Leek Town

It is reputed that Eric Skeels wrote to Stoke City manager Frank Taylor asking for a trial in the summer of 1956 while he was registered as an amateur with Stockport County. His letter was acknowledged, and during a four-week trial period at the Victoria Ground he impressed all and sundry with his enthusiasm, all-out commitment and not least his ball skills.

He was eventually signed as a full-time professional by the Potters in August 1956, and after making excellent progress in the youth and reserve teams he was handed his Football League debut in March 1960 in the Second Division home match against Charlton Athletic, when he occupied the right-half position in a 3–1 defeat.

After one more outing that season (against Hull City) Eric became a first-team regular in 1960–61, and over the next 16 years or so he amassed an exceptionally fine set of statistics. He accumulated a club record 594 first-class appearances (507 in the Football League) and scored seven goals. Taking into consideration friendly and tour matches, his overall tally of appearances for the club's first XI reached 606 and no other player to date has passed the 600 mark for the club.

He became known as 'Mr Dependable' and could play in both full-back positions and also in the right and left-half berths. He helped the club win the Second Division title in 1962–63 and finish runners-up in the League Cup in 1963–64, when the Potters were defeated over two legs by Midland rivals Leicester City. Eric, in fact, played in 38 of the 42 League games during that Championship-winning campaign and netted four goals: the point saver against Derby County at The Baseball Ground (1–1), one in each of the draws against Plymouth Argyle (2–2) and Huddersfield Town (3–3) and one in a 3–1 home win over Newcastle United. That season his half-back colleagues were usually the former Wolves duo of Eddie Clamp and Eddie Stuart, and together they made a formidable trio across the middle.

From August 1960 to May 1970, Stoke City fulfilled a total of 420 League matches and Eric played in 384 of them. He was an ever present[1] in 1961–62 and 1964–65, and missed just one match in 1965–66 and two the following season.

During his last six years at the club he spent quite a lot of time sitting on the subs' bench and was called into action as 12th man on 13 occasions, having made only four substitute appearances in his first 11 years.

Eric, who lost his place in the first team to Alan Bloor, eventually left the Victoria Ground at the end of the 1975–76 season at 36 years of age. His last outing in a red-and-white striped shirt was against Tottenham Hotspur in a First Division encounter at the Victoria Ground on 21 February, when the Londoners won 2–1. That day he deputised for John Mahoney at right-half.

After a short spell in the American Soccer League assisting both Seattle Sounders and Cleveland Stokers in the space of three months, he returned to the Potteries to sign for Port Vale in September 1976. He remained at Vale Park until May 1977, during which time he made five League appearances and netted one goal. After being given a free transfer, he agreed a short-term contract with local non-League side Leek Town.

Eric played on until he was nearly 40 and in later years ran a pub in Stoke-on-Trent. He was a frequent visitor to the Victoria Ground and then the Britannia Stadium.

Denis Smith

Born: 19 December 1947, Meir, Stoke-on-Trent

Stoke City record:
Appearances: League 406+1, FA Cup 29, League Cup 34, others 12
Goals: League 29, FA Cup 4, League Cup 5, others 3
Debut: League, 14 September 1968 v Arsenal (a) lost 1–0

Managed: York City, Sunderland, Bristol City, Oxford United (twice), West
                Bromwich Albion, Wrexham

Denis Smith, who attended Queensbury Road School and represented Stoke Boys, began his playing career with Stoke City in April 1965 and turned professional in September 1966.

So goes the legend of this tough, no-nonsense defender who regularly put his head where others feared to put their feet, that if you named a bone in the human body, the chances were that Denis had probably broken it.

An integral and often inspirational member of the side for well over a decade, Denis made his first-team debut in September 1968 and formed a strong partnership with Alan Bloor at the heart of the defence. Denis played for the Potters until May 1982 when he hung up his boots after making 482 competitive appearances for the club and scoring 41 goals – none more famous than the diving header against Leeds United in February 1974 that ended the Yorkshire side's record run of unbeaten games from the start of a season.

During his time at the Victoria Ground, Denis helped the Potters win the League Cup in 1972 and reach successive FA Cup semi-finals in 1971 and 1972, and many fans consider him to be among the club's true greats, a local legend who declined to return to the club as a manager at least twice.

Never a pretty player, Denis served as the Potters captain on numerous occasions and led by example on the field of play, never shirking a tackle and always totally committed with a never-say-die approach to the game. In fact, there weren't too many strikers who fancied playing against Denis, and there are numerous stories about his contests with some of the game's finest that will live forever in the folklore of Stoke City football club.

After playing in a third of the club's League games in 1968–69, he remained a regular in the side over the next six seasons before injuries ruined the 1975–76 campaign. After that he had four more seasons as the Potters' dominant centre-back, and although absent throughout 1980–81 he returned to the fray for one final season in 1981–82.

A full England cap eluded him, although he did represent the Football League, and at the end of his playing career he joined the coaching staff at the Victoria Ground.

Denis eventually moved into League management with York City after ending his playing career and in January 1985 guided the Third Division club to a famous FA Cup victory over Arsenal before drawing with and then losing to Liverpool in the next round. The previous season, under Denis's guidance, the Minstermen became the first English club to reach 100 points when they took the Fourth Division title in style. He left Bootham Crescent in 1987 and turned down Stoke's offer to become their new manager to take over Sunderland, who had just been relegated to the Third Division for the first time in their history.

In his first season in charge the Wearsiders won the Third Division title with a record 101 points. After some poor results, Denis was sacked by Sunderland in December 1991, but was soon back in the game as boss of Bristol City, only to resign in May 1993. He made a return to management with Oxford United the following October but was unable to save the 'Us' from relegation to Division Two. Promotion followed, but with the club £10 million in debt Denis moved on to manage West Bromwich Albion from December 1997 until July 1999.

Out of football for a while, he returned in February 2000, taking charge of Oxford United for a second time, but after saving the club from relegation he saw them go down a year later before leaving to replace Brian Flynn as manager of Wrexham. The Welsh club was placed in administration to escape its creditors, and therefore became the first to suffer a deduction of 10 points. However, Denis achieved some success by guiding the club to victory in the LDV Vans Trophy before he and his assistant Kevin Russell (another ex-Potter) were sacked in January 2007.

Frank Soo

Born: 8 March 1914, Buston, Liverpool
Died: 25 January 1991, Liverpool

Stoke City record:
Appearances: League 173, FA Cup 12, wartime 81
Goals: League 5, FA Cup 4, wartime 17
Debut: League, 4 November 1933 v Middlesbrough (a) lost 6–1

Also played for: West Derby Boys' Club, Prescot Cables, (wartime guest for Brentford, Chelsea and Everton), Leicester City, Luton Town, Chelmsford City, England (7 wartime and 2 Victory international caps)
Managed: St Albans City, Scunthorpe United, IFK Eskilstuna, Örebro SportKlub, Djurgårdens IF, Kamraterna Oddevold, IFK Norrkoping, IFK Stockholm, FF Malmö and Högaborgs BK (all Sweden), AB Copenhagen (Denmark), Israel and Sweden national teams

Frank Soo – real name Hong Yi Soo – represented Liverpool Schools and played for West Derby Boys' Club (Liverpool) before joining Prescot Cables in 1932 while working as an office clerk. He continued his office duties and made rapid progress as a scheming inside-left, so much so that he was signed as an amateur by Stoke City manager Tom Mather in January 1933, being upgraded to the professional ranks 10 months later.

Within 48 hours of signing as a full-timer he became the first player of Chinese descent ever to appear in the Football League, when he made his debut for the Potters in a Division One game against Middlesbrough at Ayresome Park. Unfortunately for Frank and his teammates, it was a happy day up on Teesside as the Potters crashed to a 6–1 defeat.

Frank made 16 senior appearances that season and scored three goals, all in January, with two coming in successive FA Cup ties against Bradford Park Avenue and Blackpool. He added nine more outings to his tally in 1934–35 before gaining a regular place in the side the following season when he was switched to the left-half position, where he would excel over the next four years and become a huge favourite with the Victoria Ground faithful.

He made 160 more appearances up to the outbreak of World War Two, being an ever present in 1937–38 and 1938–39. He was part of a brilliant half-back line with Arthur Tutin and Arthur Turner, and also with Turner or Billy Mould and Jock Kirton.

During the war, Frank guested for Everton, Chelsea and Brentford and played nine times for the England national team, lining up against Wales in May 1942, September 1943 and October 1945; versus Scotland in April 1944, October 1944, February 1945 and April 1945; against France in May 1945; and Ireland in September 1945. He also represented the FA Services XI against France and Belgium in 1944.

In September 1945, after appearing in 266 first-team games for the Potters (173 in the Football League), Frank moved to Leicester City for a fee of £4,600, rejoining the manager who had signed him for Stoke, Tom Mather. After just two FA Cup games for the Foxes, he switched his allegiance to Luton Town in July 1946 for £5,000, and after appearing in 75 games for the Hatters he took over as manager of St Albans City early in the 1947–48 season.

In 1950 he appeared in the Southern League for Chelmsford City before becoming manager of the Italian club SC Padova, a post he held until July 1952. Later that year he was appointed senior coach/manager of the Swedish side IFK Eskilstuna, taking over at Örebro SportKlub in 1953, Djurgårdens IF in 1954 and Kamraterna Oddevold in 1956.

By June 1959 he was back in England as manager of Scunthorpe United, but left the Old Showground in May 1960 after his one season in charge had seen the Iron finish a respectable 15th in Division Two. He subsequently returned to Scandinavia, taking over as coach/manager of IFK Norrkoping in 1962, IFK Stockholm in 1963 and AB Copenhagen in 1965. He later coached in Copenhagen and at FF Malmö before taking over as coach of Högaborgs BK in 1972. He also had a spell as manager of the Israeli and Swedish national teams and finally quit football in May 1974 at the age of 60.

Billy Spencer

Born:	15 May 1903, Nelson, Lancs.
Died:	Prior to 1990, Stoke-on-Trent

Stoke City record:

Appearances:	League 338, FA Cup 16
Debut:	League, 13 February 1926 v Portsmouth (h) won 2–1

Also played for: Hebden Bridge FC and Crewe Alexandra

Full-back Billy Spencer was 21 years of age when he joined Stoke as an amateur from non-League club Hebden Bridge in December 1924. He made rapid progress via the second XI and in April 1925 was handed a professional contract by Potters manager Tom Mather.

A former mill worker, Billy developed into an exceptionally fine, clean-kicking defender. Able and willing to play in both the right and left-back positions, at times he would eagerly fill in at centre-half during a match when the recognised pivot was off the field injured.

Billy was cool and calm under pressure, brainy, had superb positional sense and was good in the air, especially when defending his near post at corner-kicks. He never seemed to be tormented or teased for long spells by his opposing winger and more often than not Billy tended to get the upper hand as the game progressed. He once confessed that he never liked playing against West Brom skipper Tommy Glidden or Joe Hulme of Arsenal, both of whom were quick over the ground, but those were only two of a good many quality wingers who were playing when Billy was around.

He formed a terrific full-back partnership with Bob McGrory which spanned almost 10 seasons. In fact, they played together around 250 times between 27 March 1926 and 4 May 1935 and it was only injury and illness that interrupted this tremendous sequence.

As ever presents they played in every game (all 46) in 1927–28 and missed only one out of a possible 43 competitive matches in 1934–35, Billy being sidelined for the away clash at West Bromwich Albion on Christmas Day.

After making his debut in place of Alec Milne in a home League fixture against Portsmouth in February 1926, Billy made 16 appearances that season, and in 1926–27 he played in 36 games, helping the Potters win the Third Division North Championship.

The following season he and McGrory had that supreme unbroken partnership. In fact, goalkeeper Bob Dixon behind them missed only one game, centre-half Tom Williamson was absent twice and wing-half Harry Sellars was out of the team just nine times as the Potters came fifth in the Second Division, missing promotion by five points.

Occasionally checked on by the England selectors, Billy was unlucky not to receive an international call-up. The nearest he got to any sort of representative honour was to be put on standby for an Inter-League game, but that didn't worry him unduly. He loved his football and continued to give his best for Stoke City. He remained part and parcel of a very compact and well-organised defence and over a period of five seasons (1926–31 inclusive) missed only 13 out of a possible 210 League games.

Unfortunately, he was injured on the opening day of the 1931–32 campaign against Chesterfield at the Victoria Ground and missed the rest of the season, replaced at full-back by Alf Beachill. Billy was back in the fray in 1932–33 playing in 37 games, mainly as Beachill's partner after a leg injury sidelined McGrory. Billy gained a second League-winners' medal, this time for Second Division glory.

Billy played in the top flight for three seasons, and at times he performed as well as ever, amassing a further 90 senior appearances (87 in the League) before Charlie Scrimshaw and Ira Winstanley took over the two full-back positions. Remaining at the club for another two years as an experienced reserve, he turned out for the second XI on several occasions before eventually leaving the Victoria Ground and signing for near neighbours Crewe Alexandra for just £750 in June 1938.

Billy made a total of 354 League and FA Cup appearances for the Potters but never scored a goal. He had no reason to, really, as he probably stopped hundreds from being scored against his team!

He didn't play any sort of football during the war, officially retiring in 1940, and afterwards he chose to live in Stoke until his death.

Freddie Steele

Born: 6 May 1916, Hanley, Stoke-on-Trent
Died: 23 April 1976, Newcastle under Lyme

Stoke City record:
Appearances: League 224, FA Cup 27, wartime 95
Goals: League 140, FA Cup 19, wartime 81
Debut: League, 22 December 1934 v Huddersfield Town (a) won 4–1

Also played for: Downings Tilings, Mansfield Town (player-manager) and Port Vale (player-manager), (wartime guest for Arsenal, Bradford Park Avenue, Doncaster Rovers, Fulham, Leeds United, Leicester City, Northampton Town, Nottingham Forest, Notts County and Sheffield United), England (6 full caps)

Freddie Steele was signed by Stoke City manager Tom Mather as an amateur in 1931 at the age of 15. He worked as a junior clerk in the club's offices, trained four times a week and played for local non-League side Downings Tilings and the Potters' second team until he was old enough to turn professional in June 1933. He made his senior debut in December 1934 in a 4–1 League win at Huddersfield, and scored his first goal for the Potters four days later when West Bromwich Albion were defeated 3–0 at the Victoria Ground.

Nicknamed 'Nobby' by the fans, Freddie developed into a terrific marksman for Stoke, netting a total of 240 goals in 346 games at the club. This tally included a five-timer in a 10–3 record home League win over West Bromwich Albion in February 1937 and his haul of 33 League goals in 1936–37 remains a club record to this date.

A knee injury sidelined him for quite some time in 1937. In fact, he struggled to recover from the damage caused and decided to retire from competitive League and Cup action in May 1939, aged 23. However, he was persuaded to return to the game and was quickly back on the scoresheet, netting 10 times in five matches upon his return.

The outbreak of World War Two failed to halt his progress, and Freddie scored over 80 goals in almost 100 appearances for the Potters in various regional competitions over six years, returning to FA Cup action in 1945–46 and League football the following season. And what a terrific return he made, banging in 49 goals in 43 games during the course of that transitional season (1945–46) and following up with another 31 in 1946–47, when the Potters almost clinched the First Division Championship, missing out after losing their final game 2–1 at Sheffield United.

Freddie eventually left the Victoria Ground in June 1949, mainly due to persistent knee problems. He became player-manager of Mansfield Town and after spending two and a half years at Field Mill transferred himself to Port Vale, where he also took over as player-manager. In 1953–54 he guided the Valiants to the Third Division North title and to within one game of Wembley, seeing them lose 2–1 to West Brom in the FA Cup semi-final at Villa Park.

Having retired as a player in January 1953, he remained in charge at Vale Park until January 1957 and was in fact out of the game for five years (visiting South Africa) before returning as boss for a second spell in October 1962, and leaving for good in February 1965.

Besides his scoring exploits for the Potters, Freddie was capped six times by England at senior level. He made his international debut against Wales in October 1936 and in April of the following year was on target in a 3–1 defeat at Hampden Park when the attendance was 149,547, the highest-ever for a game of football in the UK.

Freddie netted eight goals for his country, including a first-half hat-trick in a 4–0 victory over Sweden in Stockholm a month after the Scotland game. He also represented the Football League XI against the Irish League in Belfast in 1936 and but for that horrid knee injury sustained in 1937 would surely have gained more international recognition than he did.

Uncle of the Northants and England Test cricketer David Steele, Freddie was also an enthusiastic athlete, once hurdling for Staffordshire and competing in the men's 4 x 100 yards sprint relay. He clocked 11.5 seconds for the 100 yards.

Mark Stein

Born: 29 January 1966, Cape Town, South Africa

Stoke City record:
Appearances: League 105, FA Cup 4, League Cup 8, others 17
Goals: League 54, League Cup 8, others 10
Debut: League, 17 September 1991 v Hartlepool United (h) won 3–2

Also played for: Luton Town (2 spells), Aldershot Town, Queen's Park Rangers,
                      Oxford United, Chelsea, Ipswich Town, Bournemouth (2 spells),
                      Dagenham & Redbridge

Mark Earl Sean Stein, the younger brother of the former Luton Town striker Brian Stein, had a terrific career in English football. An out-and-out striker, he scored a total of 246 goals in 649 appearances with nine clubs over a period of 24 years (1982–2006).

Lively, with a good turn of pace and strong right-foot shot, he gained England Youth honours before signing for Luton Town as an apprentice in April 1982, turning professional at Kenilworth Road under manager David Pleat in January 1984. Two years later he had a loan spell with Aldershot Town and in August 1988 was transferred to Queen's Park Rangers for £300,000, four months after helping the Hatters win the Football League Cup versus Arsenal.

Mark left Loftus Road after just 13 months, teaming up with Brian Horton's Oxford United in September 1989, and two years later he switched his allegiance to Stoke City, signed by manager Lou Macari for a fee of £100,000. Mark became an instant hit with the Potters faithful, scoring 22 goals in his first season – 17 in the Third Division and five in the Autoglass Trophy, a competition that Stoke won courtesy of Mark's splendid strike in the Wembley Final against Stockport County, which attracted a crowd of over 48,000.

Linking up superbly with Wayne Biggins, his efforts also went a long way in helping the Potters win the Third Division title that season, Mark netting crucial goals against West Bromwich Albion, Brentford and Preston at home, and Reading, Huddersfield Town and Fulham away.

The following term, when both Biggins and Dave Regis assisted him up front, Mark was an ever present and weighed in with a further 33 goals, 26 coming in the Second Division, including terrific strikes against Exeter City at St James Park (drew 2–2), in two resounding 4–0 victories over Mansfield Town at Field Mill and Chester City at the Victoria Ground, and in a 2–0 triumph at Rotherham. He also netted a beauty in a 2–1 home Autoglass Trophy quarter-final win over one of his favourite opponents, West Bromwich Albion.

After producing some tremendous form, which saw him notch eight goals in the first 12 League games of the 1992–93 season, including braces at Portsmouth (drew 3–3) and Nottingham Forest (won 3–2), Mark was surprisingly sold to Chelsea for £1.5 million. Signed by Glenn Hoddle, he certainly did well at

Stamford Bridge, scoring 25 times in 63 games for the London club and finishing up as leading striker in his first season.

Things started to go wrong both on and off the field and once former Dutch international Ruud Gullit had taken over as manager, Mark knew his time with the Blues was coming to an end. After a two-month loan spell back with the Potters (from November 1996 to January 1997) and similar stints with Ipswich Town and AFC Bournemouth, he returned to his first love, Luton Town, in July 2000 on a free transfer. Unfortunately, he struggled to do the business for the Hatters and managed only three more goals before slipping out of favour.

He chose to remain at Kenilworth Road and was appointed as the club's reserve team player-coach in May 2001, a position he held for a year before moving as a striker to Dagenham & Redbridge in the Conference. He played some excellent football at this level and averaged a goal every two games before retiring as a player in October 2003 due to a knee injury.

Mark is now Barnet's chief physiotherapist. He was appointed in June 2007, having held the position on a temporary basis during the previous season.

Willie Stevenson

Born: 26 October 1939, Leith, near Edinburgh

Stoke City record:

Appearances:	League 82+12, FA Cup 5, League Cup 5, others 2+1
Goals:	League 5, FA Cup 2
Debut:	League, 30 December 1967 v Nottingham Forest (h) lost 3–1
Also played for:	Edina Hearts, Dalkeith, Glasgow Rangers, Liverpool, Tranmere Rovers, Vancouver Whitecaps (NASL), Hellenic (South Africa)

Honoured by Scotland as a Schoolboy, Willie Stevenson played for two minor clubs north of the border, won the League title (1959) and Scottish Cup (1960) with Rangers, for whom he made 103 appearances, and represented the Scottish League before Bill Shankly paid £20,000 to bring him to Liverpool in the October of 1962.

Willie had lost his place to the brilliant Jim Baxter in the Rangers side and was contemplating a move to Australia when both Liverpool and Preston North End put in bids to sign him. Liverpool got their man, out-bidding Preston in doing so.

He made his Football League debut in the 2–1 home defeat by Burnley the following month, and scored his first goal in English football against newly promoted Leyton Orient at Anfield shortly afterwards, having a hand in two of Roger Hunt's three goals in a comprehensive 5–0 victory.

Willie duly helped the Merseysiders clinch the First Division Championship in 1964 in only their second season back in the top flight of English football. He featured in 38 of the 42 League games, thereby cementing a starting role on the left side of the Reds' midfield, which also involved the hard-working Gordon Milne and Jimmy Melia.

In 1965 Willie was a major influence as Liverpool won the FA Cup for the first time, beating Leeds United after extra-time. He played in every tie and scored the all-important second goal from the penalty spot in the 2–0 semi-final victory over Chelsea at Villa Park.

There was more silverware at Anfield the following season as the Merseysiders were once again crowned kings of England, winning their seventh League title. Willie missed just the one fixture and scored five goals. But soon after celebrating that triumph, he and Liverpool tasted disappointment when Borussia Dortmund lifted the European Cup-Winners' Cup at Hampden Park. This was the first European Final the Anfield club had reached.

In February 1967 Shankly signed 19-year-old Emlyn Hughes from Blackpool and selected him ahead of Willie at the start of the 1967–68 season. This proved to be the turning point in Willie's career. He was called on just four times that term and by December 1967 he was on his way to Stoke City, signed for £48,000 after making 238 appearances for the Reds.

A smart, intelligent footballer with good vision and excellent positional sense, Willie went straight into the team against Nottingham Forest and remained first choice for the remainder of that season, making 18 appearances. He added another 34 to his tally in 1968–69, when he occupied all three half-back positions, played at left-back and inside-left and was on the substitute's bench as well.

He was sidelined through injury for a short while but returned to action and played in 23 games in 1969–70, mainly at right-half. The following year he struggled with his form and fitness and was called into action only five times as Stoke reached the semi-final of the FA Cup but were beaten by Arsenal in a replay.

In 1971–72 Willie played in 18 competitive games, missing the League Cup Final win over Chelsea and also another FA Cup semi-final clash with Arsenal through injury. A broken leg then ruined his last season at the Victoria Ground and in the summer of 1973 he returned to Merseyside to join Tranmere Rovers, signed by his former Anfield teammate Ron Yeats. He later assisted Vancouver Whitecaps (May-September 1974) and also Hellenic (South Africa) before retiring to go into business in Newcastle-under-Lyme with another former Stoke City player, Eric Skeels.

Willie also worked briefly in the licensing trade and ran a contract cleaning company in Macclesfield, where he still lives.

Albert Sturgess

Born:	21 October 1882, Etruria, Stoke-on-Trent
Died:	16 July 1957, Sheffield

Stoke City record:

Appearances:	League 124, FA Cup 11
Goals:	League 3, FA Cup 1
Debut:	League, 4 October 1902 v Grimsby Town (a) drew 2–2
Also played for:	Tunstall Crosswells, Sheffield United, Norwich City, England (2 full caps)

Rangy and lightweight Albert Sturgess was an honest-to-goodness defender who played a hard and industrious game. A valuable utility man in an emergency, he could fit comfortably into any defensive position. He was a strong, accurate kicker and fine header of the ball, possessed wonderful anticipation, was utterly reliable and above all, he was totally committed. It was said that he always took a cold shower on a freezing day!

Nicknamed 'Hairpin' by his colleagues, he joined Stoke in July 1900 and after doing well in the reserves was promoted to the professional ranks at the Victoria Ground three months later, on his 18th birthday.

However, with so much defensive talent on display at the club he made only 12 League appearances in three seasons, and it was a good five years before he finally gained a regular place in the Potters' first team, taking over from Jimmy Bradley at left-half. He missed only one League game out of 38 in 1905–06 and likewise the following season, when sadly the Potters were relegated to the Second Division.

Playing at a lower level, Albert maintained his form and his consistency and proved to be the backbone of the Stoke defence, again missing just one League game as the Potters headed into non-League football for financial reasons. At that juncture Albert, along with several other quality players, chose to leave the Victoria Ground. He signed for Sheffield United for a fee of £1,500, having scored four goals in 135 senior games for the Potters.

The first of his four goals for Stoke had knocked Blackburn Rovers out of the FA Cup in January 1906, his second strike set the Potters on the way to a 2–0 home League win over Bolton on Christmas Eve 1906, his third helped beat Woolwich Arsenal 2–0 in a League encounter at the Victoria Ground in April 1907

and his last proved to be the winner against Leeds City at home in September 1907.

Albert settled in quickly at Bramall Lane and in his first season with the Blades made 30 senior appearances, and followed up by being an ever present in 1909–10. United's middle line of Bill Brelsford, Bernard Wilkinson and Albert Sturgess was regarded as the best in the First Division that season.

Towards the end of the 1910–11 campaign Albert made his 100th appearance for the Blades, his efforts having been rewarded in February by the England selectors, who handed him the first of his two full caps against Ireland at Derby; his second followed against Scotland at Hampden Park in April 1914 when a crowd of over 127,000 saw the Scots win 3–1.

The following season Albert collected an FA Cup-winners' medal after the Blades beat Chelsea 3–0 in what was known as the 'Khaki' Final at Old Trafford, due to the presence of so many soldiers in uniform in the near 50,000 crowd.

Albert served in the army during World War One and went on to make a total of 375 League and FA Cup appearances (plus 137 in other matches) for the Blades before leaving Bramall Lane for Norwich City in June 1923. The oldest-ever Norwich debutant and indeed player (he was 42 years and 249 days when he made his final appearance versus Millwall Athletic in February 1925), he spent two seasons with the Norfolk club, retiring in May 1925. He returned to Sheffield to open a crockery shop on Eccleshall Road, which he ran for a number of years.

Besides being a fine footballer whose career realised a total of 564 senior appearances, Albert was a useful crown green bowls player. He was almost 75 when he died in 1957.

Billy Tempest

Born:	8 January 1893, Stoke-on-Trent
Died:	Prior to 1980, Stoke-on-Trent

Stoke City record:

Appearances:	League 163, FA Cup 15, others 38, wartime 24
Goals:	League 22, FA Cup 2, others 7, wartime 1
Debut:	Southern League, 7 December 1912 v Portsmouth (h) won 2–0
	FA Cup, 10 January 1914 v Aston Villa (a) lost 4–0
Also played for:	Trentham FC, Huddersfield Town, Port Vale

Billy Tempest was only 5ft 5in tall and weighed barely 10st, yet he was as tough as any forward in the Football League either side of World War One.

He played for his local club Trentham for a season before joining the Football League's newest club, Huddersfield Town, as an amateur in July 1910. Unfortunately he never settled in Yorkshire and failed to make the Terriers' first team. As a result he returned to Trentham in February 1911 and continued to play as an amateur before eventually signing for Stoke in readiness for the start of the 1912–13 Southern League season. He made rapid progress and in March 1913 became a full-time professional at the Victoria Ground.

Billy made just four appearances in his first full term with Stoke and added 11 more to his tally in 1913–14 before finally establishing himself in the outside-left position in 1914–15. That season he was an ever present and gained a Southern League Championship-winners' medal in the process.

World War One then disrupted his and many other players' careers, and during the hostilities, when free from his army duties, Billy made just 24 appearances for the Potters.

He returned to full-time football in August 1919 and played in Stoke's first game in the Football League since April 1908, helping the team beat Barnsley 2–0 in front of 12,000 fans at the Victoria Ground. He held his place on the left wing and finished that initial post-war campaign with 37 appearances under his belt.

Quick and clever with an eye for goal, Billy was often treated roughly by the sturdy defenders who marked him, but as stated before he was a plucky, hard and competitive footballer himself and never let the fierce challenges affect his game.

In 1920–21 he had the best scoring season of his entire career, with his 10 League goals including braces in wins over Coventry City (4–1 at home) and Sheffield Wednesday (3–1 away). He also took on the responsibility of cracking in a penalty in a 3–2 victory over Barnsley in the last home game of the season.

Billy missed only 12 League games in the first three seasons after World War One, and it was a bout of flu that prevented him from playing against Notts County at Meadow Lane in November 1921, and so denied him his first ever-present campaign as the Potters gained promotion to the top flight as runners-up behind Nottingham Forest.

In 1922–23 Billy played against some of the best right-backs in England and did well despite Stoke's failure to retain their First Division status. However, the experience gained against the likes of Arsenal, Blackburn Rovers, Bolton Wanderers, Chelsea, Everton, Sheffield United, Sunderland and Tottenham Hotspur, stood Billy in good stead for another season in Division Two. Once more he played with great determination and commitment, scoring twice in 30 League and Cup games.

Perhaps surprisingly to some ardent Potters supporters, he was transferred to near neighbours Port Vale in June 1924, having scored 32 goals in 240 first-team appearances during his 12 years at the Victoria Ground.

Billy's move to the Recreation Ground was not as straightforward as it seemed. A dispute over the transfer fee led to the Football League stepping in before a mutual agreement was reached between the two clubs, with £1,000 eventually changing banks.

Billy scored three goals in his 45 outings for the Valiants before announcing his retirement in May 1925. He later worked in a pottery factory and was a regular visitor to the Victoria Ground for many years.

Ken Thomson

Born:	25 February 1930, Aberdeen
Died:	1969, Cleveland

Stoke City record:

Appearances:	League 278 , FA Cup 24
Goals:	League 6, FA Cup 1
Debut:	League, 6 September 1952 v Middlesbrough (h) won 1–0

Also played for: Caledonian Thistle, Banks o'Dee, Aberdeen, Middlesbrough, Hartlepool United

After completing his National Service in the RAF, centre-half Ken Thomson joined Aberdeen as a full-time professional in 1947 and remained at Pittodrie Park for five years, during which time he made just 52 competitive appearances.

In June 1952 Stoke City appointed Frank Taylor as their new manager (in place of Bob McGrory) and the former Wolves full-back immediately went in search of a centre-half who would allow him to switch Frank Mountford to a wing-half position.

He directed his attention to Ken, who was already considered one of the best pivots north of the border, a future Scottish international who had already been named as reserve to the senior side and for the Scottish Football League XI.

Taylor got his man, signing Ken for £22,000 in September 1952, his first major acquisition for the club. Ken went on to serve the Potters for the next seven and a half years, amassing a fine record of 302 appearances and seven goals.

A strong, commanding defender, good in the air and better on the ground, Ken made his debut against Middlesbrough soon after signing and played in all of the remaining 39 matches that season. He scored two goals, in the 1–1 draw at Aston Villa in March and in a 2–0 victory over Tottenham at the Victoria Ground two weeks later.

The confident Scot then chose to take the vital penalty on the last day of the season in a relegation battle with Derby County at the Victoria Ground. Unfortunately he missed from the spot, the Rams won the game 2–1 and the Potters went down into the Second Division. Before the kick-off, Stoke knew they required just a point to stay up above Manchester City, but sadly it all back-fired at the crucial time and they were demoted with Derby! Ken was almost in tears at the end of the game, along with his colleagues, but as veteran John McCue said 'It's a team game and we were all to blame for not staying up.'

In 1953–54 Ken missed two League games through injury and, in an emergency with Bill Finney sidelined,

he was asked to play at centre-forward in the games against Plymouth Argyle (away) and Blackburn Rovers (ome). He did exceedingly well in both, scoring twice and setting up a goal for Frank Bowyer in a 3–0 win over the latter.

A virtual ever present in 1954–55 when he was absent from League duty just once (missing the 1–1 draw at Doncaster in April), Ken celebrated his 100th appearance for the Potters with a brilliant display in a 2–2 draw at Fulham in November. The following season he missed five League games and reached the milestone of 150 League outings for the club against Barnsley in April.

Continuing to produce immaculate displays at the heart of the Potters' defence, Ken was out of League action just 11 times during the next three seasons as Stoke battled long and hard without success to get out of the Second Division.

Around this time in his career Ken's eyesight began to trouble him: he struggled to see long distances when the light started to fade. This led to him wearing contact lenses, which initially failed to cure his interrupted vision.

Nevertheless, he never let this bother him and continued to head and kick the ball as soundly and as cleanly as any other defender in the game. Stoke's new manager Tony Waddington thought otherwise, though, and after lengthy discussions he eventually sold Ken to Middlesbrough for £8,500 in December 1959, replacing him at centre-half with Ron Andrew.

Ken scored once in 90 matches during his time at Ayresome Park, where he played alongside England internationals Brian Clough, Eddie Holliday and Alan Peacock. After a series of controversial arguments with members of the staff, including his manager Bob Dennison, Ken left Middlesbrough in October 1962 to join Hartlepool United, where he stayed until May 1963 when he retired. Remaining in the North East, he died in 1969 from a heart attack while playing golf, his favourite 'other' sport away from football.

Arthur Turner

Born: 1 April 1909, Chesterton, Staffordshire
Died: 12 January 1994, Sheffield

Stoke City record:
Appearances: League 290, FA Cup 22
Goals: League 17
Debut: League, 21 March 1931 v Cardiff City (a) lost 3–2

Also played for: West Bromwich Albion (amateur), Birmingham City, (wartime
                     guest for Crewe Alexandra, Stoke City, Wrexham), Southport
                     (player-manager)
Managed: Birmingham City, Headington/Oxford United

Arthur Turner was an amateur with West Bromwich Albion before signing as a professional for Stoke City in 1930. A strong defensive half-back, good in the air and on the ground, reliable and influential, he gained a Second Division Championship medal with the Potters in 1932–33 when he was an ever present.

Subsequently appointed captain, he missed only 12 League games out of a possible 290 played by Stoke in seven years between 4 April 1931 and 12 March 1938. Quite outstanding at the heart of the defence, he went on to make 312 appearances for the Potters up to February 1939, when he was sold to Birmingham for £6,000.

Arthur's contribution in his first few months at St Andrews was not enough to prevent the Blues from being relegated, and the suspension of League football later that year seriously disrupted his career. He was 30 when war was declared, and during the hostilities he guested for Crewe, Stoke City (in 1940–41) and Wrexham while also making 200 appearances for Birmingham, leading them to the Football League South title and FA Cup semi-finals in 1946.

In February 1948, Arthur joined Southport as player-manager, making his last League outing eight months later, aged 39. Immediately appointed manager of Crewe Alexandra, he stayed at Gresty Road for three years, returning to the Victoria Ground as assistant manager to Bob McGrory in December 1951, and later working under Frank Taylor.

In November 1954, Arthur replaced Bob Brocklebank as manager of his former club Birmingham. When he took charge, Blues were 12th in the Second Division, with one away win to their name.

During the rest of the season, they lost only once more on the road, went on to score 92 goals – their best total since the 19th century – inflicted a club record 9–1 defeat on Liverpool and clinched the Second Division title with a 5–1 win at Doncaster.

The following season Arthur took Blues to the FA Cup Final (beaten by Manchester City) and in 1957 to the FA Cup semi-finals (defeated by Manchester United). Also in 1956, he became the first manager to lead an English club into Europe when Blues represented the city of Birmingham in the inaugural Inter-Cities Fairs Cup. They lost in a semi-final replay to the eventual winners Barcelona.

In January 1958 Pat Beasley joined Birmingham, believing he was to be Arthur's assistant until chairman Harry Morris told the press that he was to be joint manager. Arthur, who read of this arrangement in a local newspaper, threatened to resign but was persuaded to stay 'for the time being' before finally leaving in September 1958, taking over as boss of Headington United on New Year's Day 1959.

In those days there was no automatic promotion to the Football League; clubs had to be elected, and that depended largely on how the chairmen of other League clubs perceived them. That year, Arthur persuaded the directors to change the name of his club to Oxford United, to increase public awareness of the football team and broaden its appeal.

His key signing was 20-year-old Ron Atkinson from Aston Villa. He became captain and went on to play 560 games for the club, leading Oxford to successive Southern League titles and into the Football League in the place of Accrington Stanley, who went bankrupt in 1962. Two years later Oxford knocked Blackburn out of the FA Cup to become the first Fourth Division side to reach the sixth round. In 1965 Arthur led United to promotion from the Fourth Division and three years later saw his team win the Championship of the Third Division. Unfortunately Arthur had no money to strengthen the side and struggled with what he had. In April 1969 he became general manager, Ron Saunders taking over as manager, and in February 1972 Arthur was dismissed by Oxford, who told him they couldn't afford his services!

Arthur remained in football until the mid-1980s, scouting for Rotherham United and Sheffield Wednesday. He was 84 when he died in 1994.

Arthur Tutin

Born:	15 June 1907, Coundon, County Durham
Died:	c.1978, Stoke on Trent

Stoke City record:

Appearances:	League 183, FA Cup 15, wartime 9
Goals:	League 3
Debut:	League, 4 November 1933 v Middlesbrough (a) lost 6–1

Also played for: Bishop Auckland, Consett Town, Chilton Colliery FC, Spennymoor United, Crook Town, Sheffield Wednesday (trial), Bradford Park Avenue (trial), Aldershot, Crewe Alexandra (guest)

Arthur Tutin was a diminutive, stocky wing-half with a strong tackle and great stamina who gave the Potters 11 years' excellent service from March 1934 until his retirement in May 1945, a month before his 38th birthday.

He played as an amateur in the North East for several amateur clubs, including Bishop Auckland and Crook Town, who at the time were forces to contend with. In fact, the Bishops won the FA Amateur Cup twice in the early 1920s, just before Arthur joined them.

After unsuccessful trials at Hillsborough and Park Avenue, Arthur started his Football League career in May 1932 when he signed professional forms for Aldershot, 400 miles from where he was born. He made just 12 appearances for the Shots before transferring to Stoke City in October 1933 for an initial fee of £250, with a further £250 to follow after an agreed number of appearances. In fact, Stoke pipped West Ham United for his signature, the Hammers having watched him two weeks running at the start of that season.

Signed by manager Tom Mather, who had been monitoring his progress for a good six months, Arthur was actually bought to replace Bill Robertson who, Mather had hinted, was set to move to Manchester United. The manager simply wanted a ready replacement and Arthur fitted his requirements to a tee.

Handed his first-team debut at right-half against Middlesbrough a week after joining, Arthur didn't have the happiest of baptisms at the Victoria Ground. The Potters crashed to a 6-1 defeat and the man Arthur was marking, Bob Baxter, had a hand in four of the goals.

Arthur's first four outings for the Potters all ended in defeats, but he got over those disappointments and tasted success for the first time in a red-and-white-striped shirt when Leicester City were defeated 2-1 at the Victoria Ground on Christmas Day 1933.

He ended that season with 28 appearances under his belt and followed up in 1934-35 with another 42, missing only one League game (a 3-2 defeat by Tottenham Hotspur at White Hart Lane). He scored his first senior goal, netting the opener in a 2-0 home victory over Birmingham in early September.

With Arthur at right-half, Arthur Turner in the centre and first Harry Sellars and then Frank Soo to his

left, Stoke had a tremendous middle line in the 1930s. Week after the week, the trio produced some sterling performances and in fact the Tutin-Turner-Soo combination played together for virtually three seasons from September 1935 until March 1938, when Turner left to join Birmingham.

Maintaining his form and fitness, Arthur was an ever present in 1935-36, making a total of 47 appearances. He followed that up with 41 outings in 1936-37 (39 in the League) and another 37 in 1937-38 (34 in the League) before injuries started to creep into his game.

After just three outings at the start of the 1938-39 campaign, he was replaced in the side by Jack Bamber and soon afterwards Soo was switched to the right-half position, allowing Jock Kirton to come in on the left. Arthur slipped gracefully into the reserves, having appeared in almost 200 competitive games for the Potters in almost five years of regular first-team football.

When World War Two broke out, Arthur took employment in a munitions factory and played where and when he could, initially for the Potters, as well as assisting neighbours Crewe Alexandra as a guest. He made just nine appearances in regional games for the Potters during the hostilities before announcing his retirement from competitive football at the end of the 1944-45 season.

Arthur remained in the Stoke-on-Trent area for the rest of his life and it is believed he passed away in the late 1970s.

Alf Underwood

Born:	1 August 1867, Hanley, Stoke-on-Trent
Died:	8 October 1928, Stoke-on-Trent

Stoke City record:

Appearances:	League 115, FA Cup 16
Debut:	FA Cup, 5 October 1887 v Burslem Port Vale (h) won 1–0

Also played for: Hanley Tabernacle FC, Etruria

Alf Underwood was a hard, formidable left-back who played with great determination and commitment. Reliable to a certain degree, he did have his off days – far too many for his own good at times – and was prone to the odd mistake. Generally speaking he was a fine, capable defender who was capped twice by England, lining up in a 6–1 win over Ireland at Wolverhampton in March 1891 and against the same country in a 2–0 victory in Belfast a year later. His full-back partner that day was his club colleague Tommy Clare, while a third 'Stokie', goalkeeper Billy Rowley, played behind them.

Fair-haired, standing 6ft tall and weighing 12st, he always wore a moustache and was signed by Stoke as a full-time professional from local junior club Etruria in July 1887. Alf played in four FA Cup ties in his first season at the Victoria Ground, making his senior debut in the Potteries derby against Burslem Port Vale, which Stoke won 1–0.

He then played alongside Clare in Stoke's first-ever game in the Football League – a 2–0 defeat at home to West Bromwich Albion on 8 September 1888. He was an ever present in the side that term, playing in all 22 League outings, and he followed up with two more ever-present campaigns in 1889–90 (22 outings) and 1892–93 (26 starts). He missed only one match in 1890–91 (versus Walsall Town Swifts when he was on international duty) and was absent on four occasions in 1891–92, missing the League encounter at Everton due to his England call and the next three fixtures versus Everton (home), Blackburn Rovers (away) and Sunderland (away) after being injured playing for his country.

A very consistent footballer and dressing room comedian (when he chose to be funny), Alf was a very serious and studious man on the football pitch. He formed a terrific full-back partnership at the Victoria Ground with Tommy Clare and, in fact, the pair played together in a total of 121 matches over a period of seven and a half years, commencing in October 1887 and ending in February 1895.

Unfortunately, Alf was continually troubled with niggling knee, back and ankle injuries from 1893 onwards and effectively announced his retirement as a senior player at the end of the 1892–93 campaign when he was only 24 years of age. He was persuaded to remain as a registered player with the Potters and, although classed as a permanent reserve, he was still called-up twice for first-team duty after that, playing in the 2–1 home win over Nottingham Forest in September 1893 when David Thomson was sidelined, and against Wolverhampton Wanderers in February 1895, when he deputised for Jack Eccles in a 0–0 draw. His last appearance brought his total of senior outings for the Potters to 131, although he never scored a single goal as he hardly ever ventured over the halfway line.

A potter by trade, Alf worked in a factory after his footballing days were over, but suffered many years of poor health in the early 1900s and was almost an invalid by the time he had reached the age of 30. In July 1908 he was struck down with illness and at the time it was stated in the local press that he was virtually destitute.

A fund to support Alf and his family was established by several notables led by Denny Austerberry, who was Stoke Football Club's secretary at that time. Though chronically ill, Alf battled on gamely for another 20 years, until 1928, when he died in a Stoke-on-Trent hospital at the age of 59. The funeral of one of England's and Stoke's finest full-backs of the 1890s was attended by over 200 mourners.

Roy Vernon

Born:	14 April 1937, Ffynnongroew, Holywell, Flintshire, Wales
Died:	4 December 1993, Lancashire

Stoke City record:

Appearances:	League 84+3, FA Cup 4, League Cup 5
Goals:	League 22, FA Cup 1, League Cup 1
Debut:	League, 20 March 1965 v Wolverhampton Wanderers (a) lost 3–1

Also played for: Mostyn YMCA, Blackburn Rovers, Everton, Halifax Town, Cleveland Stokers (NASL), Cape Town (South Africa), Great Harwood and Wales (2 Under-23 and 32 full caps)

Inside-forward Roy Vernon played for Flintshire Boys, Mostyn YMCA Juniors and the Welsh YMCA, and had trials with Everton before joining Blackburn Rovers as an amateur in May 1954, turning professional in March 1955. He made his League debut at the age of 18 against Liverpool six months later – the first of 144 senior appearances for Rovers (52 goals scored).

He left Ewood Park for Everton in February 1960, the £27,000 transfer deal taking Eddie Thomas in the opposite direction. Roy was handed his first outing by manager Harry Catterick against the reigning League champions Wolves 48 hours after signing, and he went on to score 111 times in 203 games for the club, gaining a First Division Championship medal as captain in 1963. He was, in fact, Everton's leading scorer and a reliable penalty taker four seasons running (including a haul of 27 goals in 1962–63) before his perhaps surprise £50,000 move to Stoke City in March 1965.

A rather lean-looking player with an aquiline nose, Roy possessed a powerful left-foot shot, had great skill and a cool head when taking his chances. He slipped comfortably into the Potters' line up, teaming up in centre-field with Irish international Jimmy McIlroy, with another new recruit, Harry Burrows, partnering him on the left wing.

Roy scored five times in the final 10 League games of the 1964–65 season and struck 11 more goals in 36 competitive matches the following season. Unfortunately, he was dogged by injury during the early part of 1966–67, managing only 21 starts and four goals before another injury-interrupted campaign in 1967–68 when he grabbed only three goals in 23 appearances.

Over a period of 11 years, between 1957 and 1968, which included a spell in the NASL with Cleveland Stokers, Roy played in 32 full internationals for Wales and represented his country at both Youth and Under-23 levels. He won his first full cap against Northern Ireland as a Blackburn Rovers player and his last was awarded against England as a Potter.

With manager Tony Waddington making changes to his Stoke City squad, Roy was called up only 11 times in 1968–69 and, after a loan spell with unfashionable Halifax Town (January–February 1970), he left the Victoria Ground during the summer of 1970 to sign for Cape Town FC in South Africa. His record for the Potters was a good one – 24 goals scored in 96 competitive games.

Roy returned to England in August 1970 to sign for non-League side Great Harwood, where he was reunited with two of his former Blackburn Rovers teammates, Ronnie Clayton and Bryan Douglas. He eventually retired in May 1972 to run a successful antiques business. In later life, however, he suffered with arthritis in both his hip and spine. He enjoyed a bet on the horses and greyhounds and was also a heavy smoker.

Sadly, Roy died from cancer in December 1993, aged 56. His former Everton teammate Brian Labone said of him 'Taffy Vernon was about 10 stone. Wet through he looked about as athletic as Pinocchio. He was the dressing room joker – a great guy to have around, especially when morale in the camp was at a low ebb.'

Dennis Viollet

Born: 20 September 1933, Manchester
Died: 6 March 1999, Virginia, US

Stoke City record:
Appearances: League 181+1, FA Cup 9, League Cup 16
Goals: League 59, FA Cup 4, League Cup 3
Debut: League, 20 January 1962 v Bristol Rovers (a) won 2–0

Also played for: Manchester United, Baltimore Bays, Witton Albion, Linfield (player-manager), England (2 full aps)
Managed: Crewe Alexandra

One of the most prolific marksmen in Stoke City's history, averaging a goal every three games, Dennis Viollet was a goalscoring machine. Before joining the Potters in January 1962, he netted 178 goals in 291 competitive games for Manchester United, helping the Reds win the League Championship in 1956 and 1957 and playing in two losing FA Cup Finals.

As a youngster he captained Manchester Schoolboys and was capped five times by England at that level before signing amateur forms at Old Trafford in 1949. He turned professional in September 1950 and made his League debut in April 1953.

Slim and sometimes rather frail in appearance, he was blessed with lightning pace and top-quality control, and could slice through the best defence in the game like a knife through butter. His appearance was deceptive and any defender who underestimated him soon paid the price. His only discernible flaw was a lack of aerial ability, although when playing alongside the likes of Tommy Taylor at Old Trafford and John Ritchie at the Victoria Ground, this was not a problem.

Together with Taylor, he formed a lethal combination at Old Trafford and in 1959–60 demonstrated his quality by firing in 32 goals in 36 League matches, a club record which still stands today.

Dennis loved the space created by the bustling Taylor who, in turn, scored off the opportunities fashioned by his cohort, and many people thought that the pairing would be just right for England. However, national team manager Walter Winterbottom had other ideas and only selected Dennis twice for full international duty – against Hungary in 1960 and Luxembourg a year later. He scored in his second game, which England won 4–1. He also represented the Football League.

If England fans were denied the chance of seeing his great talents, United supporters faced no such deprivation in those glorious, adventurous pre-Munich days. In 1958 Dennis was one of the players who journeyed to Belgrade for the quarter-finals of the European Cup, scoring one of the goals in a 3–3 draw. Thankfully he escaped the blazing wreckage at Munich Airport with injuries which were initially thought to be career-threatening.

During the early 1960s, Busby started to create a new United team and Dennis was subsequently sold to Stoke for £25,000. He settled down quickly in his new surroundings, and in 1962–63 he top scored with 23 goals as the Potters won the Second Division title.

The following season Dennis scored 13 in League and Cup competitions, but he was annoyed not to have scored in the League Cup Final against Leicester City, which the Potters lost over two legs.

After claiming a total of 66 goals in 207 first-class appearances for Stoke and spending a short time on loan with the NASL club Baltimore Bays, Dennis moved to non-League side Witton Albion in January 1969. Seven months later he was appointed player-coach of Linfield and gained an Irish Cup-winners' medal. In July 1970 he accepted a coaching position with Preston North End, later holding a similar job with Crewe Alexandra, whom he then managed from August to November 1971.

From April 1974 to June 1977 Dennis coached Washington Diplomats, and after that was in charge of soccer classes at Jackson University and also in Richmond, Virginia. He remained in the States until his death in 1999.

Bobby Charlton said of Dennis 'I'm delighted his record has still not been broken...it's the perfect way to remember him.' Another former teammate, Jackie Mudie, said 'He was a natural goalscorer, one of the best.'

Tony Waddington

Born: 9 November 1924, Openshaw, Manchester
Died: 21 November 1994

Stoke City record:
Games managed: 701, won 241, drew 197, lost 263

Played for: Manchester United (amateur), Crewe Alexandra
Also managed: Crewe Alexandra

Tony Waddington was manager of Stoke City Football Club for almost 17 years, from June 1960 until March 1977, and during that time he guided the Potters to their only major trophy – the League Cup in 1972 – and to the Second Division Championship in 1963. He later went on to manage Crewe Alexandra from June 1979 to July 1981.

Commonly regarded as Stoke's greatest manager, he joined the club's backroom staff as a coach in 1952 and five years later was appointed assistant to manager Frank Taylor, moving into the hot seat at the Victoria Ground three years after that.

His initial task was to stop the declining fortunes of the club and to prevent relegation from the Second Division, which he did superbly well. Within two years he had turned things round, and in October 1961 he pulled off a master stroke by enticing Stanley Matthews to return to the club from Blackpool at a cost of just £2,500. He also signed several other experienced internationals, among them Jackie Mudie from Blackpool (to link up with his former Bloomfield Road colleague Matthews), Irishman Jimmy McIlroy from Burnley and goal-machine Dennis Viollet from Manchester United. The Wolves duo of Eddie Stuart and Eddie Clamp arrived as well, along with Tommy Thompson from Preston North End. The crowds flocked back to watch home games and, after years in the doldrums, Stoke City were on the march again.

Tony steered the club back into the top flight in 1963, the Potters going up as Second Division champions, a terrific way to celebrate the club's centenary season. The team played attractive football in doing so, with no fewer than 10 players appearing in 30 League games or more. Tony then established the Potters in the top flight, doing so with limited resources. He added some more new faces to his squad, including forward Peter Dobing and wing-half Calvin Palmer, and he also engaged striker John Ritchie as leader of the attack. What a buy he turned out to be – he became Stoke's top scorer with over 170 goals to his name.

Tony secured the services of England's World Cup-winning goalkeeper Gordon Banks from Leicester City for £52,000 in April 1967. He became a star performer, and in the early 1970s helped a strong, forceful and competitive Stoke side beat most other clubs in the League and reach the FA Cup semi-finals in successive seasons, when they were unlucky to be beaten each time in a replay by Arsenal. The team also won the League Cup and played in Europe for the first time in their history.

Manager 'Waddo' had a knack for squeezing Indian summers from players thought to be well past their peak, while at the same time getting the best out of home-grown youngsters, some of whom went on to become exceptionally fine players and gain representative honours.

Under Tony's astute guidance, the team earned a reputation for playing exciting, entertaining football and he continued to recruit star players. He paid a world record fee of £325,000 for another quality international goalkeeper, Peter Shilton, from Leicester City in 1974 and signed schemer Alan Hudson from Chelsea.

A pupil at St Gregory's School, Openshaw, Tony was an amateur wing-half with Manchester United before going on to play in well over 200 post-war games for Crewe Alexandra. He would have appeared in far more if it hadn't been for a knee damage sustained when serving in the navy during the 1939–45 conflict.

Tony Waddington surprisingly left Stoke after economics forced him to sell his best players, and after a decent two-season spell in charge of Crewe he returned to his beloved Stoke City as associate director of the club in 1993, a position he held until his death the following year.

Ray Wallace

Born: 2 October 1969, Lewisham, London

Stoke City record:
Appearances: League 152+27, FA Cup 5+1, League Cup 13+1, others 12
Goals: League 15, others 1
Debut: League, 13 August 1994 v Tranmere Rovers (h) won 1–0

Also played for: Southampton, Leeds United, Swansea City, Reading, Hull City,
Winsford United, Airdrieonians, Altrincham, Witton Albion,
England (4 Under-21 caps)

At first Ray was perhaps the least known of the Wallace brothers, the others being Danny and Rodney. As his career progressed, he developed into a quality footballer who went on to play for two major clubs (Southampton and Leeds United) and also appeared in four Under-21 internationals for England.

Able to play practically anywhere on a football pitch – right-back, right midfield, through the middle or on the wing – Ray began his career with the rest of his family at Southampton, signing apprentice forms for the Saints in April 1986 and turning professional two years later in April 1988.

No one ever questioned Ray's commitment out on the pitch, his enthusiasm and work rate being second to none. He replaced the injured Gerry Forrest at right-back when making his debut for the Saints in October 1989, but soon afterwards an over-zealous tackle earned him a red card in a League Cup tie versus York City. Ray went on to appear in 44 competitive games for Southampton and played four times for England's Under-21 side (against Bulgaria, Senegal, the Republic of Ireland and Sweden in 1989–90) before being surprisingly transferred to Leeds United in May 1991, signed by Howard Wilkinson for £100,000.

He never really settled in at Elland Road and made only seven first-team appearances in three seasons as well as having loan spells with Swansea City and Reading. In August 1994 he left Leeds on a free transfer for Stoke City and immediately put his career back on track, although he did not establish himself in the Potters' first XI straightaway. Indeed, he was loaned out to Hull City halfway through this first season at the Victoria Ground and if the Boothferry Park club's financial position had allowed, they may well have signed Ray on a permanent basis.

Thankfully they didn't, and in the end Ray turned out to be Hull's loss and Stoke's gain as he went from strength to strength, going on to score 16 goals in 211 senior appearances. His ability to cover every inch of the pitch, week after week, made him the perfect foil for experienced midfield playmaker Nigel Gleghorn, and Ray had an excellent 1995–96 season. Ray lost his way somewhat the following year after changing midfield partners and, along with several of his teammates, he wasn't at his best in 1997–98, when the club was plagued by a number of internal and at times external problems.

However, 'Razor', as he was nicknamed, battled on bravely, his hard running and hard tackling in midfield endearing him to the Britannia Stadium crowd. Indeed, when he was absent through injury and/or suspension, Ray was sorely missed, for he was a vital member of the team and certainly one of the first names on the team sheet for his manager.

After several solid seasons, which included several outstanding performances and some important goals, Ray started to find it increasingly tough to hold down a regular place in the Potters' first team, especially in 1998–99, yet it was clearly evident that his presence was badly missed. There is no doubt that it was a huge surprise to a lot of people when he was released by his fourth manager at Stoke, Brian Little, in May 1999, having been a registered player with the club for practically five years.

A month after leaving the Potters, Ray joined non-League club Winsford United. Later he switched his allegiance to Airdrieonians (playing in one League game in September 1999) and after that assisted Altrincham and Witton Albion, eventually retiring in 2002. Ray's career in senior football brought him 16 goals in a total of 277 games, his best years and his best statistics coming with Stoke City.

Arthur 'Arty' Watkin

Born:	12 May 1896, Burslem, Stoke-on-Trent
Died:	Winter 1965, Stoke-on-Trent

Stoke City record:

Appearances:	League 137, FA Cup 14, others 27, wartime 9
Goals:	League 39, FA Cup 13, others 25, wartime 5
Debut:	Southern League, 18 October 1913 v Llanelly (h) won 2–1
	FA Cup, 26 September 1914 v Stourbridge (h) won 11–0

Also played for: Congleton Town

Arty Watkin never played any sort of serious football until he joined Stoke as a 17-year-old semi-professional in May 1913. He had played on waste land with his mates but never considered becoming a serious footballer until he was tempted along for a trial at the Victoria Ground. He certainly impressed the watching gallery and started his playing career in earnest the very next season, when he played in seven Southern League matches for the Potters, scoring one goal in a 4-0 home win over the Welsh club Mardy in mid-April.

The following season he was a star performer, netting a total of 31 goals. Twenty-four came in 20 Southern League games, five of them in a 10-0 thumping of Ebbw Vale, while the other seven were scored in FA Cup, four on his debut in the competition when Stourbridge were thrashed 11-0.

The Potters took the Southern League Championship by storm in 1914-15, winning the trophy with a record of 17 wins and four draws from 24 games and a goal average of 62-15. Unfortunately, World War One began and Arty, with others, had to be content with regionalised football for the next four years. He joined the army and played the odd game when he could, appearing in just nine games for the Potters and scoring five goals.

With Stoke firmly established back in the Second Division of the Football League after a break of 11 years, Arty returned to competitive action for a first-round FA Cup tie with Bury in January 1920 before going on to net three times from the centre-forward position in the last 11 League matches of that season, including a brace in a 2-2 draw at South Shields.

The following campaign, fully fit and free from injury, Arty was again the club's leading marksman, this time with 16 goals, a haul that included his first two League hat-tricks in 4-0 home wins over Nottingham Forest and Leeds United in September and November respectively.

In 1921-22 Arty continued to plague defenders up and down the country with his natural pace and aggression and scored 13 times, this time from the inside-left position with Jimmy Broad leading the Potters attack and weighing in with 27. It was much the same in 1922-23, Arty notching seven goals to Broad's 26. He also assisted in many more goals for his teammates, having a hand in three of the five scored by Stoke at Blackburn in late January when the Ewood Park pitch was covered in snow.

In August 1923, completely out of the blue, Arty turned his back on the club and went into non-League football with Congleton Town. It was a shock to the players and fans alike, but Arty had his reasons for leaving – he had been under severe pressure in his work as a pottery department manager and wanted to devote more time to this line of employment rather than playing football for Stoke.

However, after a year away, manager Tom Mather persuaded the dashing goalscorer to return to the club and Arty went on playing for another three seasons. He scored three goals in 14 League games in 1924-25, played in only two matches the following season due to a knee injury and work commitments (and was joined at the club by his brother Frank), and added three more goals to his collection in six games in 1926-27, helping the Potters clinch the Second Division Championship. In fact, two of Arty's goals at the end of that term were crucial ones – the winner against Crewe Alexandra (2-1 at home) and the first in a 2-2 draw at Stockport County.

Arty's last game in Stoke's colours was against Doncaster Rovers in April 1927. Retiring as a player in the summer of 1927, he continued to work in the pottery business until 1960, and was 69 when he died five years later.

Norman Wilkinson

Born:	8 June 1910, Tanobie, County Durham
Died:	18 May 1975, Stoke-on-Trent

Stoke City record:

Appearances:	League 186, FA Cup 12, wartime 14
Debut:	League, 7 December 1935 v Wolverhampton Wanderers (h) won 4–1
Also played for:	Tanobie FC, Tannfield Lea, West Stanley, Huddersfield Town, Sheffield Wednesday (guest), Oswestry Town

Goalkeeper Norman Wilkinson had been playing football for eight years before he was signed as a professional by Huddersfield Town in May 1933 as cover for England international Hugh Turner. Although he spent two years at Leeds Road, he failed to get a game in the Terriers' first team and in July 1935 moved to Stoke City, signed for £100 by manager Bob McGrory, who had taken over from Tom Mather that summer.

McGrory's main priority was to sign a capable goalkeeper, and he had no doubt that Norman was his man, having learnt a lot about his prowess via the club's scouting network.

A former miner down a Durham pit, Norman started out as a centre-half before making over 100 appearances in goal for a strong West Stanley side over a period of three seasons. He certainly knew about the art of goalkeeping, being big and strong with a huge pair of hands. Also able to kick long and straight, he was never afraid to dive at the feet of his opponents and went on to have a fine career between the posts for the Potters.

He took over the number-one spot in the Stoke team from Norman Lewis in December 1935, making his debut for the Potters in a 4–1 home League win over Wolverhampton Wanderers. He played in a total of 30 League and FA Cup games during the second half of that season and missed only one game in each of the next two campaigns, missing out when Stoke ran up their best-ever League win when beating Staffordshire rivals West Bromwich Albion 10–3 at the Victoria Ground in February 1937, and looking on when Liverpool won 3–0 at Anfield seven months later. Doug Westland deputised for him in each of these fixtures.

An absentee on four occasions in 1938–39, Norman entered the wartime period with 156 first-team appearances under his belt, and being an experienced miner he was not called to arms by his country. This enabled him to continue playing for the Potters when he could during the hostilities. Circumstances restricted him to only 14 appearances in the six years to 1945, although he did play as a guest for Sheffield Wednesday, having seven outings for the Owls in 1943–44.

When transitional League football was introduced for all clubs in August 1945, Stoke were enlisted as members of the Northern Section, but there was no place in the first team for Norman, who found himself playing second fiddle to Dennis Herod in the Potters' goal. He remained in reserve throughout that campaign and acted as understudy during the next two as well before being recalled for a League game against Blackpool in April 1949. He played his part in a 3–2 win and, when Herod was injured during the following December's encounter with Sunderland at Roker Park, Norman reclaimed the number-one position and retained it until the end of the season.

Not getting any younger but keeping himself fit and active, he was called up for first-team duty on six occasions in 1950–51 and played in 13 League games the following season, taking his overall tally of first-team appearances for the club to a healthy 212 before leaving for non-League side Oswestry Town in August 1952.

He was 42 years of age at that time and was delighted to have given the Potters 17 years' loyal and dedicated service. At times in the mid-1930s, he was regarded as one of the finest goalkeepers in the country, one newspaper report stating that he was well worth an England call-up.

Norman, who returned to live in the Potteries after quitting Oswestry in 1953, was a fine table tennis player besides being an accomplished goalkeeper and won several minor competitions during the 1930s and 1940s. He was almost 65 years of age when he died in 1975, having been an invited guest at the Stoke City against Manchester City League game at the Victoria Ground two years earlier.

Dennis Wilshaw

Born: 11 March 1926, Stoke-on-Trent
Died: 10 May 2004, Stoke-on-Trent

Stoke City record:
Appearances: League 94, FA Cup 14
Goals: League 40, FA Cup 9
Debut: League, 9 December 1957 v Swansea Town (h) won 6–2

Also played for: Packmoor Boys Club, Walsall (on loan), Wolverhampton
                     Wanderers, England (12 full caps)

After a dubious start in which he looked anything but a future England international, Dennis Wilshaw developed into a natural goalscorer, a player who, in today's game, would have fitted into any forward line or any formation his manager or coach preferred to adapt.

Strong, determined, quick over 20–30 yards, a smart header of the ball and with a powerful shot in either foot, he had the knack of being in the right spot at the right time, finding the back of the net regularly throughout his lengthy career.

Joining Wolverhampton Wanderers as an amateur in August 1943, he made his first-team debut against Black Country rivals West Bromwich Albion in a regional wartime game the following month at the age of 17 and turned professional on his 18th birthday. He scored five goals in 13 outings during the latter part of World War Two but was loaned out to Third Division South side Walsall by manager Ted Vizard 'to gain experience at competitive level'.

Dennis found the net on his debut for the Saddlers in a 2–2 draw with Notts County, with future Wolves winger Johnny Hancocks notching the other goal. He helped Walsall reach the Final of the League South Cup that season and was an automatic choice at Fellows Park when League football resumed in earnest in August 1946.

Playing at inside-left or on the left wing, Dennis displayed excellent form throughout the 1946–47 campaign, scoring 21 goals which included the first hat-trick of his career in an 8–0 win over Northampton Town.

In his two post-war seasons at Fellows Park, Dennis notched 31 goals in 82 outings before returning to Molineux a more accomplished and certainly a more experienced player. He starred regularly in Wolves' second team before setting out his stall with a sparkling treble on his senior debut against Newcastle United in March 1949, a game broadcast on BBC radio that day, thus bringing Dennis national publicity.

Although he continued to find the net, claiming 10 goals in rapid time, he was not included in Stan Cullis's FA Cup Final team that beat Leicester City 3–1 at Wembley.

Full of confidence nevertheless, Dennis knew he had to work hard at his game as there were so many other talented forwards at the club. He finally established himself in the team and in 1953–54 gained a League Championship medal as Roy Swinbourne's strike partner.

He also won his first full England cap, scoring twice on his debut in a 4–1 win over Wales in a World Cup qualifier in October 1953. Selected in the World Cup squad for the Finals in Switzerland, he played in two games, against the host country in Group Four and versus Uruguay in the quarter-final, which England lost 4–2. In April 1955 he scored four times when England beat Scotland 7–2, becoming the first player to achieve that feat at Wembley.

With Jimmy Murray and Bobby Mason eager for first-team football, Dennis eventually left Molineux for Second Division Stoke City in December 1957 after netting 117 goals in 232 games for Wolves.

Although aged 31, he still had a lot to offer and over the next three and a half years scored almost 50 goals in 108 games for the Potters. He started out on the left wing, having a hand in three of the six goals scored by Stoke on his debut against Swansea. He struck nine times in his first season, doubled that tally in 1958–59, added a further nine in 1959–60 and notched 14 the following term. Sadly, he was forced to retire after breaking his right leg in an FA Cup tie against Newcastle United in February 1961.

A schoolteacher by profession, Dennis later became head of the service and community department at Alsager College near Crewe. A member of the ex-Wolves Players' Association, he was 78 when he died in 2004.

Charlie Wilson

Born:	30 March 1895, Atherstone, Warwickshire
Died:	15 May 1971, Stafford

Stoke City record:

Appearances:	League 156, FA Cup 11
Goals:	League 110, FA Cup 8
Debut:	League, 13 March 1926 v Clapton Orient (a) lost 4–0

Also played for: Coventry City, Tottenham Hotspur, Huddersfield Town, Stafford Rangers, Atherstone Town, Wrexham, Shrewsbury Town, Alfreton Town

Charlie Wilson remains to this day one of the most prolific goalscorers in the history of Stoke City Football Club. He netted a total of 118 goals in 167 League and FA Cup games during his five years at the Victoria Ground, and many feel that if he had arrived sooner, he would certainly have been the first player to score 200 goals at senior level for the Potters.

A dynamic, all-action centre-forward, fearless and confident with a heart of gold and seemingly boundless energy, Charlie played casual football at school and also in the army (from 1915–19) before having a brief spell with Coventry City and assisting Tottenham Hotspur as a guest in April and May 1919. He did well for Spurs in three non-competitive matches and a month later the London club signed him as a full-time professional. He made a terrific start to his League career at White Hart Lane, scoring a sparkling hat-trick on his debut in a 3–0 League win away to South Shields, when he deputised for Jimmy Cantrell.

Thereafter, Charlie remained in reserve to the England player for the rest of that season, although he was called up for another 11 outings in which he scored four more goals, including important ones against Lincoln City, Blackpool and his future club Huddersfield Town, helping Spurs clinch the Second Division title.

With Cantrell coming to the end of his career, Charlie competed with Alex Wilson for a place in the forward line over the next two years and eventually took over as leader of the attack, going on to net a total of 34 goals in 65 senior appearances before Herbert Chapman signed him for Huddersfield Town in November 1922.

Charlie was top scorer when the Yorkshire club won back-to-back League titles in 1924 and 1925 but had lost his place to George Brown by the time the Terriers were lining up their third successive Championship win.

After striking 62 goals in 107 games for Huddersfield and coming mighty close to a full England cap, Charlie joined Stoke City in March 1926 and continued to torment goalkeepers up and down the country, but his bold and brave efforts could not prevent the Potters from being relegated at the end of that season.

Nevertheless, he came out of the blocks like a man possessed at the start of Stoke's first-ever season in the Third Division and his goals (25 of them) went an awful long way in securing the Championship of the Northern Section. He carried on blasting away at the opposition, bagging another 37 goals in League and Cup action in 1927–28, 22 the following season and 19 in 1929–30 before he started to wind down with younger players waiting in the wings. Charlie's last season with the Potters brought him 11 goals (in 19 games) and his efforts were enough to see the team finish in mid-table.

With the club in financial difficulty, it was thought that Charlie should go on the transfer list in the summer of 1931. He was 37 years of age and in truth was well past his sell-by date. He still felt pretty fit, however, and chose to continue playing for another seven seasons, serving in turn Stafford Rangers, Atherstone Town, Wrexham, Shrewsbury Town and finally Alfreton Town before retiring to take over the Doxey Arms Hotel in Stafford and later becoming mine host of the Noah's Ark Inn, also in Stafford.

Many supporters from all walks of life regularly called into both of Charlie's drinking houses to have a pint and talk football, and he certainly enjoyed a chat about the good old days when he was a star performer. His career in major League and FA Cup football brought him 214 goals in 339 appearances – some record by some player.

He was 76 when he died in 1971.

ND - #0333 - 270225 - C0 - 240/170/14 - PB - 9781780911397 - Gloss Lamination